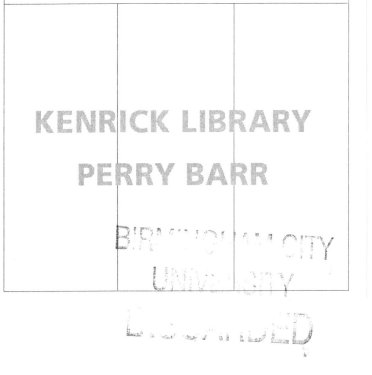

COMMUTING AND RELOCATION OF JOBS AND RESIDENCES

To Chiara, Timo and Inge.

Commuting and Relocation of Jobs and Residences

JOS VAN OMMEREN
Cranfield School of Management

Ashgate

Aldershot • Burlington USA • Singapore • Sydney

Published by
Ashgate Publishing Ltd
Gower House
Croft Road
Aldershot
Hants GU11 3HR
England

Ashgate Publishing Company
131 Main Street
Burlington
Vermont 05401
USA

Ashgate website: http://www.ashgate.com

British Library Cataloguing in Publication Data
Ommeren, Jos van
  Commuting and relocation of jobs and residences
  1. Commuting 2. Commuting - Social aspects 3. Commuting -
  Econometric models 4. Commuting - Netherlands
  I. Title
  331.2'5

Library of Congress Control Number: 00-132615

ISBN 0 7546 1042 X

Printed and bound by Athenaeum Press, Ltd.,
Gateshead, Tyne & Wear.

Contents

Preface

I became interested in studying commuting during my first job after completing my master's degree. I was amazed how many persons endured an experience that seemed to me a living hell. I thought that life has much more to offer than waiting for the next train. After years working on the subject of commuting and related topics, I realise now that I was right and that most persons try to avoid commuting. The purpose of this book is to convince readers of this important message, so often forgotten in policy debates.

Acknowledgements

I wish gratefully to acknowledge the contribution of all those who were involved in my research on job mobility, residential mobility and commuting which is reported in this book: Cees Gorter, Gerard van den Berg, Giovanni Russo and Richard Emmerink, but in particular, Piet Rietveld and Peter Nijkamp.

I wish to thank also Sarah Atterbury and, in particular, Caroline Mahoney for all their work in the preparation of the book.

I would also like to express my thanks to the following publishers for their permission to use parts of the following articles:

Blackwell Publishers for van Ommeren J.N., P. Rietveld and P. Nijkamp (1998) "Spatial Moving Behaviour of Two-Earner Households", *Journal of Regional Science*, 38, 1, 23-41.

The University of Wisconsin Press for van Ommeren J.N, (1988), "On the Job Search Behaviour: The Importance of Commuting Time", *Land Economics*, 74, 4, 526-540.

Academic Press for van Ommeren J.N., P. Rietveld and P. Nijkamp (1997) "Commuting: in Search of Jobs and Residences", *Journal of Urban Economics*, 42, 402-421 and for van Ommeren, J.N., P. Rietveld and P. Nijkamp (1999), "Job Mobility, Residential and Commuting: a Search Perspective", *Journal of Urban Economics*, 46, 230-253.

Sage Periodicals Press for van Ommeren J.N., P. Rietveld and P. Nijkamp (1999), "Impacts of Employed Spouses on Job Moving Behaviour", *International Regional Science Review*, 22, 1, 54-68.

Springer-Verlag for van Ommeren J.N., P. Rietveld and P. Nijkamp, "Job Mobility, Residential and Commuting: a Theoretical Analysis Using Search Theory", *Annals of Regional Science*, forthcoming.

PART I

STATE-OF-THE-ART

1. Introduction

Relevance of the Subject

In the last century, and particularly during the last decades, many industrialised and developing countries have encountered strong and persistent growth in commuting. The consequences of this growth on society are far-reaching in terms of congestion and other external costs such as pollution and noise. The main explanation for this growth may be found in decreased costs of travel and faster modes of transport, but other factors may also have added to this growth (e.g. suburbanisation of the population in urban areas, labour specialisation). These current historically-low costs of travel, in terms of monetary expenses and time, have produced a wide variety of commuting behaviours. Commuters strongly differ from each other in many ways. First of all, commuters differ with respect to their mode of transport (Meurs, 1991); in the second place, commuters differ widely in their commuting time or commuting distance.

Several explanations have been offered to clarify the observed differences in commuting. These theories are based on the notion that the commuting journey allows persons to spatially link their workplace and residential location. For example, this has induced labour economists to presume that commuting costs are compensated for by higher wages (Cogan, 1981) and urban economists to presume that commuting costs are compensated for by lower housing prices (see the seminal contribution by Alonso, 1964). It has also been noticed that observed differences in the value attributed to time help to explain commuting behaviour which may depend on the household situation. So observed differences in commuting are generally interpreted as a sign that commuters vary with respect to their labour position, household situation, demand for housing, accessibility to different modes of transport, etc.

Although the observed differences in commuting are partially explained by the differences in the characteristics of commuters, a robust but striking result is that empirical studies fail to explain the major part of the observed differences in commuting (White, 1986). One explanation

3

might be that many influential explanatory variables are excluded in the empirical analysis. A more satisfying interpretation is that due to market imperfections, workers do widely differ from each other with respect to commuting. Conventional urban economic models ignore the importance of market imperfections and have therefore, been severely criticised. For example, Hamilton (1982) suggests that a random matching of jobs and workers in urban areas is closer to the reality of urban commuting than the standard urban economic model with decentralised employment.

In this study, we will focus on two types of market imperfections which may have a significant influence on commuting behaviour: imperfect information and moving costs.[1] Imperfect information is included within this study by assuming that jobs and residences are search goods. Workers search over job and residence opportunities and move from job to job, and from residence to residence. With moving costs, we refer to the monetary and non-monetary costs due to moving residence or job.

In a hypothetical economy without market imperfections (perfect information, no moving costs), workers would adjust their residence or workplace location so that the costs due to commuting are fully compensated for (Alonso, 1964). In an economy with market imperfections this will rarely be the case (Weinberg, 1979; Zax, 1991; Hamilton, 1982, 1989; Rouwendal, 1994). As we wish to study the effect of market imperfections on commuting behaviour, we will focus in our study upon both the decision to move job and the decision to move residence. The decisions to move job and the decision to move residence are closely related dynamic discrete choices, as both moves involve a change of commuting costs. This means that labour and residential moving and commuting behaviour are mutually dependent and must ideally be analysed together, and based on a theory which incorporates these decisions explicitly. We have made this interdependency the core of our study.

The main objectives of this study can be summarised as follows:

(*i*)   to formulate models based on search theory in order to analyse the relationship between job mobility, residential mobility and commuting; and

(*ii*)   to use these models for empirical research concerning job mobility, residential mobility and commuting.

These objectives lead to the formulation of a number of research questions in this study:

What is the effect of commuting on job and residential moving behaviour? (see chapters 3 and 6). What is the relationship between job and residential job mobility? (see chapter 3). What is the effect of market imperfections in the housing market (e.g. residential moving costs) on job mobility? (see chapter 5). Will market imperfections increase the commuting distance? Do persons who work in "flexible" labour markets (characterised by a high probability of being fired) commute more or commute less than those who work in less flexible labour markets? What is the marginal willingness to pay to avoid an increase in the commuting distance? (chapter 7). How do two-earner households differ in their spatial moving behaviour from one-earner households? (chapters 4 and 8). Do commuting costs affect search intensity in the labour and housing market? (chapter 11). Finally, what is the relevance of this study for policies which aim to reducing commuting (road pricing, reimbursement of travel expenses)? (chapter 12).

The empirical analysis is based on data for the Netherlands, therefore, in order to provide an empirical framework for our analysis, we will highlight important facts and figures of Dutch commuting behaviour. It must be noted here that it is generally believed that commutes are shorter in the Netherlands than in other European countries. However, this belief is false. In fact, the Dutch commute more (see, Jansen, 1992).

Commuting Behaviour: Facts and Figures

The most important components of commuting behaviour are:

1. the commuting distance;
2. the commuting time;
3. the travel mode.

Information on commuting distance, commuting time and travel mode in the Netherlands is reported in the so-called Enquête Beroepsbevolking, which was conducted in 1992 (EBB, 1992). This survey is representative for the Dutch population.

In the EBB (1992), commuting distance is measured in 4 classes. We know whether the commuting distance of individuals inquired is smaller than 8 kilometres, between 8 and 16 kilometres, between 16 and 32 kilometres, or more than 32 kilometres.

Table 1.1 Frequencies of commuting distances in the Netherlands, 1992

0 - 8 km.	8 – 16 km.	16 - 32 km.	> 32 km.
0.49	0.26	0.15	0.10

    As can be seen in Table 1.1, about 50% of all workers in the Netherlands commute less than 8 kilometres.

    The EBB survey also includes information about commuting time (in minutes). When commuting time exceeds 60 minutes, however, precise information about commuting time is absent. The frequency table appears to be the following:

Table 1.2 Frequencies of commuting times in the Netherlands, 1992 (minutes)

0-10 m.	10-20 m.	20-30 m.	30-40 m.	40-50 m.	50-60 m.	> 60 m.
0.21	0.34	0.16	0.16	0.07	0.01	0.06

    As can be seen in Table 1.2, more than 50% of all workers in the Netherlands commute less than 20 minutes. The number of workers who commute more than 60 minutes is relatively small (6% of all workers). The commuting time depends, of course, on the travel mode. We will distinguish between the use of the car, bicycle, train, public transport (excluding train) and by foot.[2]

Table 1.3 Frequencies of travel modes in the Netherlands, 1992

Car	Bicycle	Public transport.	Foot	train
0.54	0.32	0.06	0.04	0.04

More than 50% of all commuters travel by car.[3] However, almost one third of all commuters in the Netherlands chooses the bicycle. In the Netherlands, policies have mainly been used to influence the choice of the travel mode. Remarkably, policies which are introduced to restrict the commuting distance or commuting time are largely absent (an exceptions is the duty on gasoline).[4] So, a priori, it seems that policies should also stimulate workers to commute less (distance or time). Several policies which may reduce the costs of commuting may be envisaged:

- road pricing and other policies which increase the costs of commuting. The use of this type of policies is, however, politically very sensitive (Verhoef, 1996);
- the introduction of telematics systems (Emmerink, Nijkamp and Rietveld, 1996; Nijkamp, Pepping and Banister, 1996);
- policies which stimulate workers to change job or residence. For example, a priori, one may expect that a reduction of the residential relocation costs may stimulate workers to change residence in order to commute less. This kind of policy may be quite effective in combination with other measures (such as road pricing). According to Tables 1.1 and 1.2, commuting distances and commuting times are not evenly spread among workers: a small share of the employed causes a relatively large part of all commuting costs to society (e.g. congestion). Thus, policies which cause a relatively small share of workers to commute less, may have a significant effect on the total costs of commuting to society. This may justify the current study of the relationship between job mobility, residential mobility and commuting.

Outline of this Study

In light of the aforementioned research aims, the study will be divided into five parts. Part I will give a short state-of-the-art review of research into commuting and moving behaviour. Part II will deal with the relationship between job and residential mobility and commuting from a theoretical point of view. Part III will present the results of an empirical analysis of job and residential mobility in the Netherlands. In part IV, we will discuss empirical analyses of commuting and on-the-job search behaviour. Part V concludes in the remainder of this chapter, the contents of these five parts will be summarised.

Part I. State-of-the-Art

In the first part of the study (chapter 2), we give a short state-of-the-art review of the developments in commuting and mobility research. This review is by no means comprehensive, but it is the foundation for our assertion that it may be fruitful to analyse commuting behaviour from a dynamic perspective.

Part II. Theory

In chapter 3, an analytical search model is introduced which aims to highlight the relationship between job mobility, residential mobility and commuting. This model is developed on the basis of recent developments in search theory. An essential element of the model is that it does not rely on any sequential ordering of job or residential moves. One of the basic implications of the model is that workers with relatively high commuting costs tend to expect that those costs are only temporarily borne. It is also argued that the model indicates that workers first accept a job and then move residence closer to the new workplace location, although this sequence may be reversed, depending on specific conditions of the labour and housing market.

Chapter 4 extends the search model introduced earlier. Here, we focus on the relationship between job mobility, residential mobility and commuting of two-earner households. The case of two-earner households deserves special attention, because the two wage earners in the same household share a dwelling but have different working places, which adds to the complexity of the spatial decision problem. We demonstrate that the distance between the workplaces of the two wage earners may play a key role in order to understand the spatial moving behaviour of two-earner households. In chapter 5, we focus on the impact of market imperfections and geographical structure on commuting behaviour.

Part III. Empirical Application of Moving Behaviour and Commuting

Our analysis of job mobility and residential mobility is carried out by employing Dutch data at the micro level in chapter 6.

In chapter 7, we lay the foundation of a procedure to estimate the workers' marginal willingness to pay for commuting based on the search model proposed in chapter 3. We demonstrate that given information on job durations and voluntary job moves, the marginal willingness to pay for commuting can be empirically estimated.

Chapter 8 and 9 draw attention to the empirical investigation of job moving behaviour of two-earner households. The Telepanel (1992) data set provides unique information on two-earner households which enables us to test some of the theoretical predictions of the search model.

Part IV. Empirical Applications of Commuting and On-the-Job Search

Chapter 10 is the empirical counterpart of chapter 5, in which the effect of market imperfections on commuting is examined. The Enquête BeroepsBevolking (1992) data set provides information regarding the on-the-job search activities of those who are employed. In chapter 11, we investigate empirically whether employed persons vary job search behaviour with respect to commuting distance, commuting time and mode of transport. One of the (surprising) outcomes is that search intensity does not depend on the mode of transport.

Part V. Summary and Conclusions

In part V, the approach chosen in this study is evaluated and conclusions are drawn - on the basis of the theoretical and empirical results.

This study provides a theoretical and empirical investigation of job moving, residential moving and commuting behaviour in the Netherlands in which the emphasis is on the dynamic aspects. This approach provides new insights into the relationship between commuting behaviour and the functioning of the labour and housing market.

This kind of research may be of relevance for effective commuting policies, because it provides a theoretical and empirical foundation for the notion that commuting policies which aim to reduce commuting affect the functioning of the labour and housing market. For example, we find that those with longer commutes search significantly more in the labour market, and change more often job and residence. The theory presented in this study strongly suggests that the expectation of costly future job or residential moves prevents workers from reducing current commuting distance. Welfare losses due to commuting might therefore be reduced to a certain extent by fiscal measures which reduce the costs of moving job. For countries with rigid housing markets (such as the Netherlands), it may be also beneficial to introduce measures which increase the flow rate of moving residence.

Notes

[1] In this study, market imperfections are defined as those factors which inhibit individuals to move to the optimal location.

[2] Whenever workers use several travel modes (e.g. bicycle and train), information about the main travel mode is included.

[3] The car is especially chosen to commute distances between 8-32 kilometres.

[4] Some tax-policies even stimulate commuting. For example, those who commute more than 10 km may deduct a part of the travel costs from the tax bill.

2. A Review of Commuting, Job Mobility and Residential Mobility Research

Introduction

The main objectives of this study is to investigate the relationship between commuting and mobility behaviour in the labour and housing market. The specific objective of this chapter is to give a short review of (separate) developments in commuting and mobility research.[1] Initially we will focus on theoretical commuting models and furthermore we argue that it is worthwhile to analyse commuting behaviour from a dynamic perspective, as a job move and a residential move may imply a change of commuting distance. Next, we review the empirical commuting literature. Finally, we concentrate on job and residential relocation behaviour - particularly in relationship to commuting. It will be established that a general theoretical framework which describes commuting behaviour must preferably include the determinants of both residence and job relocation.

Commuting Behaviour: Theoretical Models

Many studies have attempted to answer the following question: given the characteristics of an individual, where would this individual locate his/her residence given the workplace location? Economic theories have contributed a valuable answer to this question. Assuming the existence of a simplified static world with perfect markets, a utility maximising individual accepts the costs of the work trip, because the marginal commuting costs are compensated for by marginal benefits. In other words, the commuter accepts the disutility of commuting, because the commuter is compensated by either higher wages or cheaper housing. Based on the compensating principle, various approaches are plausible for analysing commuting behaviour. In this section, we will discuss approaches which have originated from research fields such as urban economics, housing economics and labour economics.

Urban Economics

Models in urban economics are based on the assumption that firms and households compete for scarce land for production and housing activities. The underlying behaviour is thought of as bidding behaviour. Following the tradition of Alonso (1964), these urban models contain a typical structure of the urban area. Traditionally, the urban area contains only one centre in which employment is concentrated and land prices decrease gradually from the centre to the rural areas. Employees may choose to locate near the centre (enjoying low commuting costs, but expensive housing) or locate farther from the centre (enjoying higher commuting costs, but cheaper housing). The model has been extended towards more realistic applications, including decentralised employment (inclusion of wage gradients) and several business centres (Muth, 1969; White, 1988). The assumptions of the spatial structure of the urban area are obviously restrictive which limits a general application of this model. For example, the structure of land use in the Netherlands may be described as multi-centred (Clark and Kuijpers-Linde, 1994). These centres are not only relatively small, but are also not too far from each other. Outside the centres therefore the density of housing and production is also high and not monotonically decreasing. The standard urban economics model also assumes that markets are perfect, and has therefore been heavily criticised (Anas, 1982; Hamilton, 1982, 1989). In this study, market imperfections will obtain due attention.

Housing Economics

The location of the residence determines the length of the commuting journey. So in the field of housing economics, it is thought that longer commuting journeys are compensated for by lower housing prices (ceteris paribus). By observing the prices of different houses one may, in principle, calculate the implicit price of commuting. A complicating factor is that houses differ in aspects other than their location. Housing is a typical example of a composite good. A dwelling can be described by a number of characteristics which all contribute to the value attached to the complete dwelling. The various aspects of the good housing cannot be bought separately. They obtain their proper value only in combination with the other characteristics. The hedonic price is the maximum offer price of the household, as well as the minimum asking price by the landlords. The standard reference to the estimating procedure of hedonic price equations is Rosen (1974).[2]

Kim (1992) attempts to disentangle demand and supply interpreting the hedonic price equation differently. He views the hedonic equation as the minimum asking rent by the landlords which determines the competition among landlords. A housing demand function takes into account the search process for a suitable housing unit. Since the search activities are not observable, the observed transaction data in a housing market are truncated. Hence the standard housing demand model would suffer from truncation bias. His model provides a joint estimation of the hedonic price and housing demand (reservation rent) equations. One of his interesting results is that commuting time is significant in the jointly-estimated model. As a consequence, estimation of hedonic price equations based on search behaviour seems promising.

Labour Economics

Wales (1978) formulates a labour supply model which incorporates commuting time in a utility maximisation framework where persons have to decide how much to commute. Housing prices are assumed to vary with commuting time. He reports estimates which imply that commuting time is valued at an average of about two-thirds of the wage rate.

According to the labour market theory of equalising differences, an equilibrium locus of wage and job characteristics exists and can be estimated by an appropriately specified wage equation.[3] Thus a hedonic wage equation representing the worker's marginal willingness to pay for non-wage characteristics can be estimated. Commuting can, nevertheless, hardly be regarded as a fixed non-wage job characteristic, as the worker may alter the commuting distance by moving residence (Zax, 1991b). In addition, hedonic wage theory has severely been criticised, as it would render negatively biased estimates (Gronberg and Reed, 1994). We return to this problem later.

In the studies that make use of static models, imperfect information and moving costs are ignored. Under these assumptions, workers would adjust their residence or workplace location so that the costs due to commuting are fully compensated. In an economy with market imperfections, however, this will rarely be the case (Weinberg, Friedman and Mayo, 1979; Zax, 1991b; Holzer, 1994).[4] For example, rental housing markets are sometimes heavily regulated, as is the case in the Netherlands. In addition, in most countries, a tax must be paid when buying a dwelling (in the Netherlands, this tax is about 6%). These factors distort dwelling price adjustments and prevent households from moving. Therefore, concern may be expressed about the pitfalls of modelling the decision of where to locate residence given the workplace location, or when estimating the relationship between commuting distance and housing prices in the Netherlands.

This suggests that a better understanding of commuting behaviour may be obtained by focusing on search behaviour and market imperfections. Although we hypothesise the importance of market imperfections on commuting behaviour, we realise that factors such as imperfect information and moving costs are very difficult to observe. These factors are, however, directly related to moving behaviour which one may observe. To improve understanding of the effect of market imperfections on commuting behaviour, we will shift our focus towards job and residence moving behaviour. Job and residential mobility has increasingly become a topic of interest as it enables the researcher to study varieties of market imperfections (search costs, uncertainty, moving costs). This study will build upon current knowledge gathered in the fields of job and residential mobility.

Summary

In conclusion, we have briefly reviewed existing theories of commuting behaviour. These theories are particularly relevant when analysing commuting behaviour in areas with a simple spatial structure, but are difficult to apply in general. Current theories have recently been criticised, as they ignore the consequences of market imperfections such as moving costs and uncertainty, and therefore, of moving behaviour. Before we review the developments in mobility research, we will focus upon empirical commuting research.

Empirical Commuting Research

Empirical commuting research has concentrated on a number of interrelated research topics. In the United States, the effect of the metropolitan spatial structure on commuting behaviour has received considerable attention (Hamilton, 1982, 1989; Gordon, Kumar and Richardson, 1989).[5] Gordon, Kumar and Richardson (1989) report that polycentric and dispersed metropolitan areas facilitate shorter commuting times. The study by Clark and Kuijpers-Linde (1994) supports this conclusion for the Randstad (the western part of the Netherlands). The city size and degree of suburbanization, however, do not appear to affect the commuting distance in the Netherlands (Rouwendal and Rietveld, 1994).

The mode of transport chosen by the commuter continues to be an interesting research topic for the Netherlands (Meurs, 1991; Meurs, Kockelkoren and Jager, 1991; Meurs and Bovy, 1992; Clark and Kuijpers-Linde, 1994). An interesting finding is that the choice for a certain mode is very stable for most individuals; many commuters do not change mode even when they alter work or residence (Pbivvs, 1992).

A number of studies has examined which characteristics influence the length of the journey-to-work (measured in distance or time). A general result is that commuting decreases as a person ages (Rouwendal and Rietveld, 1994; Camstra, 1994). Educational achievements tend to increase commuting distance (Rouwendal and Rietveld, 1994). The numbers of hours worked and the influence of the wage or income have received some attention. According to the monocentric urban model, it is expected that a higher income increases commuting distance; according to the polycentric model, however, such a relationship is not expected and also not found (Gordon, Kumar and Richardson, 1989). It is noteworthy that for most commuters, it may be reasonable to assume that the (accepted) wage, mode of transport and commuting time are simultaneously chosen, contingent upon the residential location. Female commuters with a partner are however more likely to work part-time and it is then reasonable to assume that the number of hours worked interferes with the accepted commuting time (Rouwendal, 1995).

The general notion that women commute less is supported by most empirical studies, although this effect may be negligible if women were in the same situation as men (e.g. same wage, number of hours, same mode of transport see Madden, 1981). It is often thought that commuting behaviour strongly depends on the position of the worker in a household and the type of household. Empirical investigations of commuting behaviour of single wage-earners and two-earner households do not however render conclusive results (White, 1986; Madden, 1981 for the U.S.; Rouwendal and Rietveld, 1994, for the Netherlands).

According to a number of empirical studies, commuting behaviour is affected by the length of the time spent in the current job and residence (and thus by job and residential moving behaviour) (White, 1986; Madden, 1981;

Singell and Lillydahl, 1986; Dubin, 1991). In these empirical studies, a variety of effects are reported. White (1986) finds that residence tenure has a significant negative effect on commuting. Madden (1981) finds negative effects for job tenure.[6] Singell and Lillydahl (1986) find that in two-earner households that recently have changed their residence, male commute times decline whereas female commute times increase. These effects may reverse when female earnings exceed males. Dubin (1991) reports that residential mobility has relative little importance on the extent to which workers use firm decentralisation to shorten their commutes, but job mobility is important. Rouwendal and Rietveld (1994) find that starters on the labour market have an above-average commuting distance. Finally, the studies of Dubin (1991) Siegel (1975) and Simpson (1980) support the hypothesis that the employment location is more responsive to the residential location than the residential location is to the job location (due to high residential moving costs).

Until now, we have focused on theoretical and empirical commuting research. We have argued that commuting behaviour is affected by market imperfections and consequently by job and residential moving behaviour. In the current section we have reviewed the empirical literature. It has indeed been found that job and residential moving behaviour has some effect upon commuting behaviour. In the next section, we will focus on job and residential moving behaviour.

Moving Behaviour

In this section, we discuss job and residential moving behaviour, particularly in relationship to commuting. First, we will review the literature on job moving behaviour; then we will review the literature on residential moving behaviour; finally, we will review the literature which addresses job moving and residential moving behaviour simultaneously.

Job Moving Behaviour

We will focus here on search theory which attempts to explain job moving behaviour.[7] We will concentrate on search theories which explicitly include commuting. We will not discuss those mobility theories which aim at understanding migration behaviour to other regions with better job opportunities (e.g. the migration model of Sjaastad, 1962) which is based on human capital theory). Although these theories often explicitly contain a spatial dimension, they typically do exclude commuting behaviour.[8] Another reason not to discuss migration theories is because it is of relatively minor importance in the Netherlands. Furthermore, *empirical* studies of net migration conclude that migration due to increased job opportunities does only occur at a limited scale in the Netherlands. We will report here some evidence of this outcome: interregional *net* migration has often been explained by labour market equilibrating forces acting to equalise wage differentials and overall economics conditions among various areas (Greenwood, Mueser, Plane and Schlottmann, 1991). Participants on the labour market migrate because of differences in wages between regions (neo-classical motives), or because of differences in unemployment between regions (Keynesian motives). In the Netherlands, however, migration flows are almost perfectly symmetric: immigration and emigration are almost in balance for each region, so net migration is almost negligible (Evers and van der Veen, 1986). This is remarkable because differences in labour market conditions between regions in the Netherlands are not completely absent. A tentative explanation would be that the limited supply of houses affects migration (Evers and Van der Veen, 1983). Nijkamp and Rietveld (1982) also report that the housing market (and the environment) affects migration flows, but that the condition on the labour market has no effect on net migration. Bartels and Liaw (1983) find that labour market conditions such as unemployment may affect migration Finally, the study of Van Dijk, Folmer, Herzog and Schlottman (1989) did not find that unemployed migrate more often than employed.

Stigler (1961, 1962) introduced the concept of search in economic models. The core of this concept is that economic actors search for goods on the basis of uncertain and limited knowledge and it is assumed that offers are stochastic. In essence, search theory implies that the decision-maker maximises lifetime utility under uncertainty. McCall (1970) showed under which assumptions the utility maximising decision-maker searches sequentially. The basic search model has been extended in several ways. For example, variable search effort, moving costs and non-stationarity have been included in the model (McKenna, 1985; Devine and Kiefer, 1993; Mortensen, 1986).[9] Recent developments in search theory emphasise that a job move is the result of a match between job seekers and employers (Pissarides, 1994).

Job search theory has been originally developed to understand the search behaviour of unemployed persons. So job search theory has been chiefly used to explain the dynamics of unemployment. A number of studies also aim to understand on-the-job search (Burdett, 1978; Black, 1981; Hall, 1982; Hey and McKenna, 1979; Holmlund and Lang, 1985; Hughes and McCormick, 1985; Kahn and Low, 1982, 1984; Mortensen, 1986; Hartog, Mekkelholt and Van Ophem, 1988; Hartog and Van Ophem, 1994; Van Ophem, 1991; Lindeboom, 1992; Van den Berg, 1992, 1995; Pissarides and Wadsworth, 1994; Burgess, 1992).

We note the following differences between 'on-the-job search' and 'unemployed search'. First, it has been generally observed that unemployed searchers tend to accept nearly all job offers. This does not hold for employed searchers (Mekkelholt, 1993). Second, employed searchers receive job offers even when they do not search (Hartog, Mekkelholt and Van Ophem, 1988).[10] Furthermore, several theoretical contributions can be found in the literature in which it is argued that the on-the-job-search costs are small, but job moving costs may be considerable (Hey and McKenna, 1979; Hughes and McCormick, 1985; Van den Berg, 1992).

In the labour market literature almost all emphasis has been on wages, while spatial aspects are of less importance. Similarly, in the job search literature there is scarcely any literature that addresses the *location* of the job; most study the search behaviour of job seekers. Notable exceptions are Sugden (1980), Simpson (1980), Van den Berg and Gorter (1996), Rouwendal and Rietveld (1994), Holzer (1994) and Rouwendal (1995).

Sugden (1980) was one of the first who recognised that search theory is well-suited for handling problems of the spatial dimension of labour markets. He defined the net wage of a job as the wage earned minus commuting costs and showed that an increase in the cost of travel implies an increase in the reservation wage. Simpson (1980) developed a theory of the workplace location from a predetermined household location by concentrating on spatial job search. His starting point was to test the statement of Siegel (1975) that 'the employment location appears to be more responsive to the home location than the residential location is to the job location'. One of the observations which confirms this statement is that the job moving costs are expected to be smaller than the residential moving costs for most commuters. Our finding in this study that the commuting distance negatively depends on the probability of moving job, but does not depend on the probability of moving residence may support this statement.

Simpson's (1980) model of workplace choice extends the theory of job search by explicitly considering the spatial dimension of job search.[11] The searcher samples jobs of which the attributes are unknown, so he will sample more in areas close to his residence because of the higher time and commuting costs. So the standard job search assumption that jobs arrive completely at random and are exogenous to the job seeker is dropped.

Holzer (1994) discusses how the urban geography of employers and residences may affect job search behaviour. An important outcome is that suburbanisation by firms seems to particularly affect those who are most restricted in the housing market. Rouwendal and Rietveld (1994) examine the influence of commuting distance on the acceptance of a job in the absence of moving costs. The reservation wage (the minimum wage asked which induces job acceptance) can then be calculated as the sum of the minimum wage asked for were commuting costs absent plus the commuting costs. Van den Berg and Gorter (1996) derive the job acceptance strategy for unemployed persons who may move residence once. Finally, Rouwendal (1995) concentrates on the acceptance strategy of unemployed Dutch women.

In this study we are concerned with the effect of commuting costs on job moving behaviour. Empirical studies have included measures for commuting costs as a cause of job mobility. Van den Berg (1992) reports that individuals with longer commuter distances are more willing to change jobs. The results of Mekkelholt (1993), however, do not indicate a positive significant relationship between commuting time and the probability of accepting a job. Van den Berg and Gorter (1996) find that the reservation wage of an unemployed seeker increases if a job is offered at a larger commuting distance from the current residence.

Van Ophem (1991), Mekkelholt (1994) and Hartog and Van Ophem (1994) examine the decision of whether or not to search. They include, among a range of other variables, commuting time as a factor which may influence this decision. The results of Van Ophem (1991) show that commuting time significantly increases the probability an employed person searches for another job, but the results of Hartog and Van Ophem (1994) find only weak effects. According to Mekkelholt (1994), the empirical results refute the hypothesis of a significant relationship between commuting time and the search decision, because those with higher commuting costs usually have higher wages which sufficiently compensate for the commuting costs.

Residential Moving Behaviour

We will now discuss different theories which attempt to explain residential moving behaviour. Residential mobility (including migration) has received much attention by geographers and economists for a long time (Ravenstein, 1885).[12] We will not discuss the literature on migration, as residential relocations over large distances are often a result of a job move.[13]

Initially, short-distance mobility research has proceeded along non-economic lines (Rossi, 1955; Shaw, 1975). Geographers and sociologists considered economic factors of limited use to analyse short-distance mobility. They stated that the homo economics is not the sensible explanation of human behaviour in a spatial context. Mobility research was theoretically improved by Wolpert (1965), who introduced the concept of 'place utility', related to the concept of 'bounded rationality' of Simon (1957). Wolpert defined place utility as 'the net composite of utilities which are derived from the individual's integration at some position in time'. This includes all costs and benefits which related to a certain location. The individual becomes interested in moving if a certain dissatisfaction threshold level is reached. This threshold is some function of his experience (life cycle) or attainments at a particular place.

Economists were initially interested in long-distance migration where economic motives dominate. When they became interested in residential mobility in the 1970s, they criticised the work that had been done. For example, Weinberg (1979) claimed that earlier researchers when examining residential mobility earlier researchers, neglected important economic factors such as the effect of workplace changes on the household's decision to move its residence.

In the residential mobility literature, it has been specifically recognised that discrete changes in the characteristics of the household play a major role in the residential moving decision; for example, the birth of a child changes the demand for housing (Graves and Linneman, 1979).[14] Individuals may move their residence because of a changing demand for a non-traded location-dependent good (in general, the characteristics of a house are fixed). Shifts in demand for traded goods will generally not result in changing the location, because relocation implies large monetary and non-monetary costs. A relocation can also be motivated by a change in demand for location specific goods which does not depend on the characteristics of the house such as improvement of environment or improvement of social contacts (VanderKamp, 1972; on return migration). So residential mobility is particularly determined by 'sociological' determinants, while typical 'economic motivations' are often absent. Relocations over shorter distances are primarily caused by changes over the life-cycle, especially when they are associated with a change in the composition of the household (birth of child, divorce), or a change in income. For an investigation of residential mobility in the region of Amsterdam (Rima and van Wissen, 1987).

In this study we are especially concerned with (changes in the) commuting costs which will affect residential mobility. Changes in the commuting costs that are exogenous have been studied (e.g. a workplace relocation by the employer, Engelsdorp Gastelaars and Maas-Drooglever Fortuijn, 1985; Zax, 1991a; Holzer, 1994; Van Wee, 1996). The effect of a change in the commuting costs which are not exogenous but are instead endogenous due to a voluntary job move have also received attention in the literature. (Weinberg, 1979; Verster, 1986; Gleave and Cordy-Hayes, 1981). For example, Verster (1986) finds that residential moves are still triggered by a workplace change after a considerable time lag.

It has been observed that residential moves may also occur which are not related to any change in a characteristic of the household (or environment). We offer two types of explanations. The first is that the willingness to move is a function of the resistance to leaving the present residence (habit forming) and the accumulated stress or dissatisfaction with the present residence. Both the resistance to moving and dissatisfaction with the current residence (residential stress) tend to increase with increasing length of stay in the same residence (Clark, Huff and Burt, 1979).[15] Another explanation is that households aim to improve their position by searching for residences, because they realise that there are dwellings superior to the one they now occupy. This will be particularly important in markets which are heavily regulated and/or in markets with low residential flow rates. The search process may however also be of importance in case that characteristics change. For example, the (expected) birth of a child may increase the demand for space, so the household will search for larger dwellings. Conceptually, the search processes in the housing and labour market are similar, including the decision to search, the search process and the decision to accept an offer.[16] Similar to the labour market literature, search behaviour in the housing market has received some attention (Brown and Holmes, 1971; Speare, Goldstein and Frey, 1975; Clark and Flowerdew, 1982; Clark and Van Lierop, 1986; Clark and Smith, 1982; Huff, 1984; Pickles and Davies, 1991; Rouwendal and Rietveld, 1988; Smith and Mertz, 1980; Smith, Clark, Huff and Shapiro, 1979; Smith and Clark, 1982; Wheaton, 1990; Kooreman and Rouwendal, 1992; Rouwendal, 1991, 1992).

Lack of information and costs of sampling are at the heart of the search process of these studies. In more formal search papers, it is assumed generally that the distribution of place utilities is known. The assumption that sampling is costly seems very sensible, because of monetary and time costs. Note however, that the costs of moving are not included in these studies, whereas the costs of moving may be of more importance than the costs of search. The costs of the search and the expected gains of searching clearly diverge among households. For example, Speare, Goldstein and Frey (1975) examined the time spent searching for a house before one moved. He reported that owners did not search more often than renters but while they were searching, on average they searched longer. Rouwendal (1991) provides empirical evidence that many households accept a type of house which is not their first choice. This could lead one to the conclusion that, for them, waiting longer is too costly.

Although the importance of commuting costs has been emphasised in the residential mobility literature, in the theoretical residential search literature, commuting costs have been largely ignored (exceptions include Huff, 1984; Rouwendal, 1992).

Residential and Job Moving Behaviour

The mobility theories we have reviewed until now implicitly assume a sequential ordering of the decision to move or to change jobs (except Zax, 1991a). Either individuals search for jobs from their homes (residence-dominance theories), or individuals locate their homes implicitly near their employment location (workplace-dominance theories). These theories may not adequately or correctly describe the actual mobility decisions of households with respect to commuting. These theories ignore that the commuting distance can be varied by changing job or residence. Models which encompass both processes are preferred. It seems therefore useful to describe the decision-making process as if the decision to move residence and the decision to move job are dependent (Siegel, 1975; Steinnes, 1977; Simpson, 1980; Beesley and Dalvi, 1974; Bartel, 1979; Weinberg, 1979; Linneman and Graves, 1983; Evers and Van der Veen, 1985; Zax, 1991a, 1994; Zax and Kain, 1991; Van Wissen and Bonnerman, 1991; and Waddell, 1993). Although these studies use different methodologies, they conclude that the decision-processes on the labour and housing market are related.[17]

In this study we hypothesise that residential and workplace relocation influence each other because of the occurrence of commuting costs. A change in the commuting costs due to a workplace relocation leads to an inducement to transfer the residential location, and vice versa. Contrarily, workplace relocation and residential relocation may be substituted one for the other.[18]

To analyse simultaneous decision taking in both markets, one may begin from the assumption that the household is in equilibrium with regard to location and quantities of housing services consumed. So the household regards its current consumption of housing, commuting and choice of job as optimal. The household considers a relocation only when exogenous changes occur which affect the relative desirability of all locations and quantities. Alternatively, one may suppose that commuters are not in equilibrium, for example, because of moving costs, imperfect information and search costs. These market imperfections make it dubious to assume that simultaneous mobility actually takes place, even though the decisions about mobility are made simultaneously. Moreover, households expect changes in the future which will affect the decision-making now (See for example Hardman and Ioannides, 1995; who investigate the effect of expected wage increases on residential mobility in the presence of moving costs). As a consequence, forward looking behaviour with respect to job and residential mobility might be of importance. Hence in this study, instead of assuming the absence of market imperfections, we explicitly recognise the importance of market imperfections and forward looking behaviour. Search theory might be an appropriate tool to analyse job and residential mobility, as it enables the researcher to study the effects of market imperfections on commuting behaviour (see also Rouwendal's, 1992; study of search behaviour in the housing and job market).

Conclusion

We conclude that given the absence of market imperfections, commuting behaviour might be explained by static theories. Market imperfections such as moving costs and uncertainty are, however, generally prevalent. This means that labour and residential moving and commuting behaviour are mutually dependent and must preferably be simultaneously analysed by using a theory which incorporates these decisions. We have made this interdependency the core of our study. In Chapter 3, a search model is introduced which incorporates labour mobility, residential mobility and commuting.

Notes

[1] We will focus on disaggregated models, particularly micro-economic models, as in research areas related to commuting (labour market, migration and housing market research). In the last decade attention has shifted from aggregated models towards disaggregated models. We will follow this trend. Moreover, this review does not claim to be comprehensive, but it does address the main developments.

[2] If housing prices and all housing characteristics are observed, one could discover the determinants of demand and supply for dwellings. These observations cannot however solely identify demand and supply determinants. The *net* value of commuting distance could therefore be implicitly calculated, but the value of commuting to the workers remains unknown. The method of implicit pricing is valid under the assumption of full competition. The Dutch housing market may hardly be characterised however by pure competition which leads Verster (1986) to doubt whether there is an unambiguous relationship between prices and housing characteristics in the Netherlands. On the other hand, the assumption of no relationship whatsoever between commuting and housing prices seems implausible. It is further noted that the distance to employment centres is correlated with many other variables (e.g. amenities like fresh air and other environmental benefits) which are difficult to measure. As a consequence, whether an approach based on hedonic prices would give sensible results in the Netherlands is questionable. The only attempt known to us to estimate hedonic price functions for the Netherlands is the study of Rouwendal (1991) which does not include any information about the commuting distance-price relationship.

[3] According to Kasper (1983), employers pay higher wages to those who commute farther.

[4] To understand the effect of market imperfections on commuting, one may use static models, but it is unclear whether is it possible to obtain interesting results which do not strongly depend on the assumptions of the geographical structure.

[5] In micro-behaviour studies, the distribution of employment and housing are given. However, the spatial structure of the area reveals firms' and households' location preferences (Muth, 1969; Steinnes, 1977) ; Greenwood, 1980). In the United States, the location of labour force members in the suburbs appears to have encouraged the growth of the housing stock and suburban employment (see Greenwood, 1980).

[6] Tenure is the time spent in a certain state (e.g. job or residence).

[7] Other labour market theories which attempt to explain job mobility concentrate on wage growth as the main determinant of job mobility. Commuting costs are included as a non-wage characteristic which may influence job satisfaction (Mekkelholt, 1993). Mekkelholt (1993) contains an extensive description and explanation of labour mobility in the Netherlands. For a comparison of international job-to-job rates, see Van Ours (1990).

[8] This seems to be a plausible approach, because if differences are large between regions in terms of job opportunities, then the distance between these regions is generally too far to commute.

[9] Since the beginning of the 1980①s, interregional migration analysis has been integrated into job search theory (Miron, 1978; Rogerson, 1982; Pickles and Rogerson, 1984; Maier, 1987; Weibull, 1978; Clark, 1987; McCall and McCall, 1987). An assumption underlying these models is that labour markets are spatially distinct, which does not apply for the Netherlands where spatial labour markets tend to be partially overlapping.

[10] Further, an unemployed person has no commuting costs, whereas an employed person has.

[11] Moreover, the model attempts to incorporate the concept of heterogeneous labour in terms of the conventional elements of human capital, namely levels of schooling and job training or

work experience. He argues that skilled workers will search over a wider spatial extent, as they are more specialised and have to examine more jobs.

[12] Note that in the residential mobility literature it is quite common to make a distinction between intra-regional and inter-regional mobility (migration). The difference between intra-regional and inter-regional relocation is not of importance in this study, so we shall not distinguish between these types of relocations. In a few typical cases, we shall recall the difference between interregional and interregional relocation, if necessary.

[13] Most residential relocations are over small distances. For example, in the Netherlands the average distance between the old and the new residence is 4.2 kilometres, while 75% of all residential moves is less than 15 kilometres (Van Dijk, 1986).

[14] Note that in the labour market, cumulation of human capital is a continuous process.

[15] McGinnis (1969) was one of the first to develop a statistical model which explicitly models attachment to a place. He incorporated time dependencies, viz duration of residence. In the 1970s, economists became interested in the effect of housing tenure. See, in particular, the work of Ginsberg (1979a,1979b).

[16] A large difference is that bargaining about the housing price plays an important role, while in the labour market bargaining about the wage occurs to a lesser extent (see Burdett and Wright, 1992; Van Ommeren and Russo, 1995).

[17] For example, Van Wissen and Bonnerman (1991) find that a job relocation triggers a residential move, which in turn has a diminishing effect on the likelihood of changing work in the near future. Evers and Van der Veen (1985) conclude that migration and commuting are often substitutes: when a job move takes place over distances less than 80 kilometres, commuting is more 'attractive' than migration.

[18] This has been shown to occur when commuting costs change exogenously as the employer relocates. In the case of significant relocation costs, the individual will choose between one of the relocations and will not change both (Zax, 1991a).

PART II

THEORY

3. Job Mobility, Residential Mobility and Commuting: Search Theory

Introduction

Theoretical and empirical mobility studies suggest that residential and job mobility intensities vary according to the level of commuting distance. In general, higher commuting distance tends to make workers more willing to move workplace or residence. Since commuting distance changes after a residential or a job move, job and residential mobility are mutually dependent (see, inter alia, Bartel, 1979; Linneman and Graves, 1983; Zax, 1991; Van Wissen and Bonnerman, 1991). Although the relationship between job and residential mobility and commuting distance is evident, a general conceptual framework in the economic literature which encompasses job mobility, residential mobility and commuting distance is still lacking (see Zax, 1991; 1994) for a recent contribution employing static choice theory). Such a general framework can be helpful in analysing the potential effects of policies which affect commuting behaviour. For example, in many large urban areas, the price of commuting might rise due to increased congestion costs. One might expect this to affect the choice of the residential and workplace location, and consequently to alter the dependency of residential and mobility behaviour. A theoretical model may then help predict the effects or interpret results of empirical studies. Interpretation of the estimated effect of commuting distance based on partial job or residential mobility studies is tedious, since it is often neglected that commuting distance changes endogenously.

Current theories which explain job and residential moving behaviour generally rely on a sequential ordering of the decision to move residence or to change jobs: individuals search either for jobs given their residence (Sugden, 1980; Simpson, 1980; Rouwendal and Rietveld, 1994;

Van Ophem, 1991; Van den Berg, 1992). Or individuals search for a new residence given the workplace location (Weinberg, 1979; Weinberg, Friedman and Mayo, 1981; Smith and Clark, 1982; Clark and Flowerdew, 1982; Huff, 1984; Pickles and Davies, 1991; Rouwendal, 1991). A theory which does not depend on such a sequential ordering is useful, because we are better able to understand the interaction between the activities of individuals on the labour and housing market. Present studies on the relationship between job and residential mobility are often based on static equilibrium models in which unexpected shocks and life-cycle changes play a key role (Weinberg, 1979; Linneman and Graves, 1983; Zax and Kain, 1991; Zax, 1991).[1] Although interesting for specific situations, the existence of large once-only moving costs will generally imply that commuters exhibit forward looking behaviour, which is captured by dynamic theories. In this paper we will provide a search framework which enables us to analyse the relationship between residential and workplace relocation behaviour. So we derive the optimal strategy and show the comparative statics results. We find that the effect of factors which cause housing market imperfections (viz. the residential moving costs and the residence arrival rate) have ambiguous effects on the job acceptance and job search behaviour of *employed* individuals. Under specific conditions however, the effect of housing market imperfections on labour market behaviour of employed persons can be determined. Nevertheless the effect of housing market imperfections on the labour market behaviour of *nonemployed* persons can be derived. Those persons who are nonemployed will accept fewer job offers and search less intensively in the labour market when residential moving costs are higher.

The outline of the paper is as follows. First, we introduce a search framework which includes search in the labour and housing market. Second, we derive the optimality conditions. Then we focus on the optimal strategy and the relationship between job and residential mobility, we report on the comparative statics of the model. Finally, we discuss the general belief that workers first move job and then move residence, and we interpret such a belief based upon our model.

A Search Framework

Our objective is to derive a theoretical framework which explains the on-the-job and residential relocation behaviour of full-time employed individuals who explicitly take into account commuting distance. The relationship between job mobility, residential mobility and commuting distance will be described from a search-theoretical perspective. Search theory is appealing as it is based on the primary idea that individuals maximise utility by moving through different states and so it is explicitly dynamic. We make the assumption that job and residence offers arrive exogenously at a specified rate and that these offers are instantly accepted or rejected. So job and residential moving behaviour are due to a combination of chance - the arrival of an offer - and a decision-making process - the decision to accept an offer. Although some might argue that these assumptions seem rather far-fetched, we think that such a description reaches the heart of the matter; it seems unlikely that anyone is able to precisely choose the optimal amount of commuting distance (See Alonso, 1964; Zax, 1991; for contrasting assumptions).

For more than a decade, job search theory has been one of the main theoretical and empirical tools for understanding the working of the labour market. In their overview paper, Devine and Kiefer (1993) conclude that much more attention should be paid to nonwage characteristics, such as commuting distance. Although theoretical job search models exclude the impact of residential (re)locations, the effect of the residential location is included in empirical applications. For example, several empirical applications of job search theory point to significant effects of commuting distance. Van Ophem (1991) reports that the search decision of workers is positively related to the commuting time. Van den Berg (1992) concludes that one is reluctant to give up the advantage of short travelling times between home and work, which has a significant influence on job mobility. Although search theory has been less influential in explaining residential mobility behaviour, researchers have become increasingly interested. In conclusion, we argue that job mobility, residential mobility and commuting distance are mutually dependent, thus a model which includes these elements may be significant.

In principle, search theory can readily be applied to determine the optimal decision rule of moving job and residence: individuals are thought of as facing a set of alternative dwellings and a set of alternative employment opportunities. Every combination of dwelling and job location uniquely determines the commuting distance. The costs and benefits of any dwelling or job offer are examined, with regard to potential future dwelling and job offers. These costs and benefits are a function of many characteristics, including personal and household characteristics, current job and dwelling characteristics and commuting distance. Macro factors like job availability and housing supply also play an important role, as these factors determine whether better combinations of dwellings and jobs can be found.

A standard point of departure in the search literature is the distinction between the rate that a job or residence is offered, the so-called arrival rate, and the probability that the offer is accepted. In the job search literature, most results stem from the basic principle that jobs are characterised by wages and that workers prefer higher wages.[2] In the residential mobility literature, the basic principle is that individuals prefer a higher *place utility* to a lower place utility, where place utility is defined as the utility experienced in a certain location (net of housing costs), which depends on the specific benefits of the residential location (Wolpert, 1965; Yapa, Polese and Wolpert, 1971).

Whether an individual accepts a residence or job offer not only depends on the direct gain in wage or place utility, but also on the *once-only costs associated with moving* and the *search costs*. The once-only costs associated with moving residence consist of costs like notarial and real estate agent charges, furnishing of the new dwelling, and the effort of moving (or fees for the mover); whereas the once-only costs associated with moving job consist of items such as the loss of retirement pension in the Netherlands and fringe benefits. Of course, the once-only costs also include psychic costs. As far as we know from the literature, no clear empirical estimates of the level of generalised costs of moving residence are available, but these costs are likely to be high (Boehm, 1981; Amundsen, 1985; Ioannides, 1987; Pickles and Davies, 1993). In contrast, the results of Van den Berg (1992) show that the exit rate from the job is hardly influenced by the cost of quitting, which might be an indication that job changing costs are low. In our search model, we have explicitly included the once-only costs associated with moving job and residence. Initially we will ignore search costs, as it has been argued elsewhere that on-the-job search costs are modest for most professions (Hey and McKenna, 1979; Van den Berg, 1992), whereas the search costs for a new residence compared to the once-only costs of moving residence are expected to be small. We assume that every worker is continuously engaged in search for a better residence and a better job.

The typical situation in which a worker searches continuously for a job given fixed turnover costs has been explored by Hey and McKenna (1979). They suppose that when workers evaluate a job offer they contemplate the notion of moving more than once in the future. So the difference between the new wage offered and the present wage needs to be *greater* than the costs of moving 'to guard against the possibility of getting another offer after moving that would have been preferred before moving, but which is not sufficiently high to induce a second change'. As a consequence, the more *moves* one expects, the larger this difference will be, because one does not want to pay too many times for the costs of moving.

Van den Berg (1992) has extended this on-the-job search model by allowing the once-only costs of moving to depend on the current wage earned which may vary. The insights offered by this extended search model also increase our understanding of residential mobility behaviour: the once-only costs associated with moving to another dwelling depend strongly on the type of the tenure chosen (renting, owning). This extended model predicts that the type of tenure chosen is simultaneously determined with the expected number of moves.

In the search models known to us, mobility in another market is ignored. The acceptance probabilities of jobs and dwellings however depend on each other, as a job or residence relocation implies a change of commuting distance which affect both acceptance probabilities. Application of the concept of search theory suggests that if individuals search on both markets, they will accept a dwelling or job offer only when the expected gains of an offer are higher than an acceptable minimum, taking into account future offers on *both* markets. The properties of the optimal strategy of the worker who faces job and residential offers may thus shed new light on the relationship between job and residential mobility and commuting. In line with the current search literature, we will derive a search model assuming that workers consider commuting distance and the once-only costs of changing jobs and residences in their search for jobs and dwellings.

Finally, it is worthwhile to mention that the model can easily be extended by incorporating varying search effort in the labour and housing market and by including more than one wage earner. For reasons of clarity, we do not discuss such an extension here. In addition, we omit mathematical proofs.

Job and Residence Search: The Optimal Strategy

The point of departure in this section is that individuals are employed and search continuously for better jobs and dwellings. Individuals derive utility from the wage w, place utility r and commuting distance z (an alternative interpretation is to interpret z as commuting time). So, the instantaneous utility v experienced in a certain period of length Δt by an individual is a function of w, r and z and is equal to $v(w,r,z)\Delta t$.

We assume that $\partial v/\partial w > 0$, $\partial v/\partial z < 0$ and $\partial v/\partial r > 0$. Hence, instantaneous utility is increasing in wage and place utility, and is decreasing in commuting distance. The individual takes into account the once-only costs of changing jobs c_1, and residences c_2. Furthermore, for convenience of notation, we suppose that the instantaneous utility v depends linearly on the moving costs c_1 and c_2. So $v(c_1 + \delta_1, c_2 + \delta_2) - v(c_1,c_2) = -\delta_1 - \delta_2$. We assume that individuals receive job and residence offers which arrive according to a Poisson process. Jobs arrive with arrival rate p_1, dwellings arrive with arrival rate p_2. This implies that the occurrence of a job offer and the occurrence of a dwelling offer are independent, which is plausible as for most professions the supply side of the labour and the housing market function operate independently.[3] Moreover, we will assume that pooling of offers is not allowed: job and dwelling offers have to be refused or accepted before other offers arrive.

A job is entirely characterised by the wage, w, and the commuting distance, z. Wage and commuting distance offers are random drawings from a bivariate distribution F_{wz}. So, w and z may be dependent.[4] Similarly, a dwelling is entirely characterised by the place utility and commuting distance, and place utility and commuting distance offers are random drawings from a distribution F_{rz}. r and z are also allowed to be dependent. The wage w is received until a new job is accepted; similarly, the place utility r is experienced until the individual changes residence.[5] The commuting distance z, is borne until the individual leaves either the job or the residence. We suppose that w, r and z assume non-negative values. The maxima of w, r and z are denoted as $\bar{w}$, $\bar{r}$ and $\bar{z}$ respectively.

Finally, we take into account that the worker may be fired at rate γ. We suppose that a nonemployed person receives a benefit of value b. Furthermore, we suppose that the costs of becoming re-employed are zero.[6] When nonemployed, the person continues searching for better work and residence alternatives. We suppose that he/she receives offers from the distributions F_{wz} and F_r respectively, where F_r denotes the marginal distribution function of F_{rz} introduced above.

For an employed person, we denote the (discounted) expected lifetime utility (indirect utility) received from the current wage, place utility and commuting distance as $V(w,r,z)$. Similarly, the value of nonemployment is denoted as $U(b,r)$. V and U include the possibility of better offers in the future. All benefits - w, r and b - and costs - z, c_1 and c_2 - are discounted at rate ρ. The individual is assumed to maximise lifetime utility $V(w,r,z)$ respectively $U(b,r)$. The basic decision the individual has to take is whether to accept a new job or a residence offer, taking into account the expected offers in the future. Consider a (short) interval of time length Δt. The lifetime utility for an employed person is then:

$$V(w,r,z) = \frac{1}{1 + \rho\Delta t}[v(w,r,z)\Delta t + p_1\Delta t E \max[V(w_x, R, Z) - C_1, V(w,r,z)]$$
$$+ p_2\Delta t E \max[V(w,r_x, z_x) - c_2, V(w,r,z)] + \gamma\Delta t U(b,r)$$
$$+ (1 - (p_1 + p_2 + \gamma)\Delta t)V(w,r,z) + o(\Delta t)].$$

In this expression the expectation is taken with respect to the variables which got a subscript 'x'. So, given a job offer, the expectation is taken with respect to the distribution of the wage and commuting distance; given a residence offer, the expectation is taken with respect to the distribution of the place utility and commuting distance. The interpretation of the above formula is straightforward. The instantaneous utility $v(w,r,z)$ is proportional to the length Δt of the time interval. With probability $p_1\Delta t$ ($p_2\Delta t$) a job (residence) offer will be received, and that offer will be accepted if the value of the new position exceeds that of the current position. If the offer is rejected, the individual's position does not improve and he/she receives $v(w,r,z)$. If the job is accepted, one has to pay moving costs. With probability $\gamma\Delta t$ the worker will be fired and become nonemployed. When nonemployed, the individual has lifetime utility U. With probability $1 - (p_1 + p_2 + \gamma)\Delta t$ the worker will neither receive a job offer nor receive a residence offer nor will be fired. The last term reflects the notion that as Δt approaches zero any nonproportionality of utility to the length of the time interval goes to zero at an even faster rate (Albrecht, Holmlund and Lang, 1991). The latter term includes the probability of receiving more than one job offer or receiving more than one residence offer since they go to zero at a faster rate. Furthermore, it is important to note that the last term also includes the probability of receiving a simultaneous job and residence offer as this probability also goes to zero at a faster rate (see for a similar proof given a more basic job search model Mortensen (1986);[7] Similarly, the lifetime utility of an nonemployed person can be written as:

$$U(b,r) = \frac{1}{1 + \rho \Delta t} [v(b,r,0)\Delta t + p_1 \Delta t E \max[V(w_x,r,z_x),U(b,r)]$$

$$+ p_2 \Delta t E \max[U(b,r_x) - c_2, U(b,r)] + (1 - (p_1 + p_2)\Delta t)U(b,r) + o(\Delta t)].$$

From now on, we will treat the workers decision problem in continuous time to simplify the analysis. So, we rewrite V and U, dividing by Δt, and let Δt approach zero. This gives:

$$V(w,r,z) = \frac{1}{\rho} [v(w,r,z) + p_1 E \max[V(w_x,r,z_x) - c_1, V(w,r,z)]$$

$$+ p_2 E \max[V(w,r_x,z_x) - c_2, V(w,r,z)] + \gamma U(b,r) - (p_1 + p_2 + \gamma)V(w,r,z)]$$

$$U(b,r) = \frac{1}{\rho} [v(b,r,0) + p_1 E \max[V(w_x,r,z_x),U(b,r)]$$

$$+ p_2 E \max[U(b,r_x) - c_2, U(b,r)] - (p_1 + p_2)U(b,r)].$$

Following Albrecht, Holmlund and Lang (1991) we rewrite the above formulae in order to prove that these formulae define the value of V and U. Let us choose a constant $M > p_1 + p_2 + \gamma$. Multiplying the above formula by ρ, adding $MV(w,r,z)$ ($MU(b,r)$) to both sides, and dividing through by $M + \rho$ gives the following expressions:

$$V(w,r,z) = \frac{1}{M + \rho} [v(w,r,z) + p_1 E \max[V(w_x,r,z_x) - c_1, V(w,r,z)]$$

$$+ p_2 E \max[V(w,r_x,z_x) - c_2, V(w,r,z)] + \gamma U(b,r) + (M - p_1 - p_2 - \gamma)V(w,r,z)]$$

and

$$U(b,r) = \frac{1}{M + \rho} [v(b,r,0) + p_1 E \max[V(w_x,r,z_x),U(b,r)]$$

$$+ p_2 E \max[U(b,r_x) - c_2, U(b,r)] + (M - p_1 - p_2)U(b,r)].$$

The above formulae define the value of V, U and the optimal acceptance rules. It is then straightforward to show that V is increasing in w and r, but decreasing in z; U is increasing in b and in r. Furthermore, the above formulae imply that V and U are both increasing in p_1, p_2 and decreasing in c_1, c_2 and γ.

The acceptance rules for individuals who search simultaneously in two markets (in the current paper in the labour and housing market) are different from those who search in one market, because acceptance behaviour in one market affects acceptance behaviour in the other market. In the current paper, individuals receive offers from a market which imply a change in the commuting distance and which therefore change the strategy in the other market. So, the optimal strategy in one market is conditional on the commuting distance offered (Van den Berg and Gorter, 1997). The following arbitrary decision rules will be proposed which states which job or residence offer induces a job or residence move, and which not:[8]

Decision Rule for the Employed:

Given a job offer of wage w_y and commuting distance z_y, and given the current wage w, place utility r, commuting distance z, and reservation wage $res_w(w,r,z|z_y)$:

change job   if $w_y > res_w(w,r,z|z_y)$
                 otherwise do not change job.

Given a residential offer of place utility r_y and commuting distance z_y, and given the current wage w, place utility r, commuting distance z, and reservation place utility $res_r(w,r,z|z_y)$:

change residence   if $r_y > res_r(w,r,z|z_y)$
                 otherwise do not change residence.

Decision Rule for the Nonemployed:

Given a job offer of wage w_y and commuting distance z_y, and given the current benefit b, place utility r and reservation wage $R_w(b,r)$:

accept job   if $w_y > R_w(b,r|z_y)$
                   otherwise do not change job.

Given a residential offer of place utility r_y and given the current benefit b, place utility r, and reservation place utility $R_r(b,r)$:

change residence   if $r_y > R_r(b,r)$ otherwise do not change residence.

These decision rules define the dynamic maximising problem because the individual maximises the lifetime utility by choosing *optimal* values for res_w, res_r, R_w and R_r. The optimal values can be established by straightforward application of standard solution techniques to derive the optimal strategy of individuals (Albrecht, Holmlund and Lang, 1991; Burgess, 1992; Hey and McKenna, 1979). First, one determines the value of the lifetime utility $V(w,r,z)$, given the current values of w,r and z and the arbitrary decision rules:

$$V(w,r,z) = \frac{1}{M+\rho} [v(w,r,z) + p_1 \int_0^{\bar{z}} \int_{res_w(y)}^{\bar{w}} [V(x,r,y) - c_1 - V(w,r,z)] \, dF_{w,z}(x,y)$$

$$+ p_2 \int_0^{\bar{z}} \int_{res_r(y)}^{\bar{r}} [V(w,x,y) - c_2 - V(w,r,z)] \, dF_{r,z}(x,y) + \gamma U(b,r) + (M - \gamma) V(w,r,z)].$$

Similarly, one may derive $U(b,r)$:

$$U(b,r) = \frac{1}{M+\rho} [v(b,r,0) + p_1 \int_0^{\bar{z}} \int_{R_w(y)}^{\bar{w}} [V(x,r,y) - U(b,r)] \, dF_{wz}(x,y)$$

$$+ p_2 \int_{R_r}^{\bar{r}} [U(b,x) - c_2 - U(b,r)] d \, F_r(x) dx + MU(b,r)].$$

The objective of the individual is to maximise lifetime utility. So, we derive the first and second-order conditions for the optimal decision rules. Setting the derivative of V with respect to res_w and res_r equal to zero gives two first-order conditions, which determine the optimal strategy for the employed. Setting the derivative of U with respect to R_w and R_r equal to zero gives the two other first-order conditions. Taking the derivative of V with respect to res_w and res_r, and setting the resultant equal to zero gives the following result:

$$V(w,r,z) - V(res_w(z_y), r, z_y) + c_1 = 0,$$
$$V(w,r,z) - V(w, res_r(z_y), z_y) + c_2 = 0,$$

where res_w and res_r denote now the *optimal* reservation values. These expressions have a clear interpretation. The former equation may be interpreted as follows. The reservation wage is chosen, conditional on the commuting distance offer z_y, such that the lifetime utility associated with the optimal level of the reservation wage which induces a job movement is equal to the cost of moving to another job plus the lifetime utility associated with the current job, place utility and commuting distance combination. The latter equation has a similar interpretation; the reservation place utility is chosen, conditional on the commuting distance offer z_y, such that the lifetime utility associated with the optimal level of the reservation place utility which induces a residential movement is equal to the cost of moving to another residence plus the lifetime utility associated with the current job, place utility and commuting distance combination. It can be easily shown that the second-order conditions for res_w and res_r are ensured.

The optimal strategy for the nonemployed is similarly determined by the following two first-order equations:

$$U(b,r) - V(R_w(z_y), r, z_y) = 0,$$
$$U(b,r) - U(b, R_r) + c_2 = 0,$$

where R_w and R_r denote now the optimal reservation values. The second-order condition is again guaranteed. Interpretation of these first-order equations is similar to the first-order condition of employed persons. The only difference is that the reservation place utility of the nonemployed is, of course, not conditional on the commuting distance offer. Clearly, according to the four first-order conditions, res_w, res_r, R_w and R_r are mutually dependent. Hence, the values of res_w and R_w do not only depend on the characteristics of the labour market, but also on the characteristics of the housing market. For res_r and R_r holds the same. As a consequence, the search model justifies the common practice to incorporate housing market characteristics in labour market models.

We have established above that lifetime V is increasing in w and r, but decreasing in z. These results rely on the assumption that the instantaneous utility is increasing in w and r and decreasing in z. Changes in the combination of w, r and z which do not affect the instantaneous utility v, may however still affect lifetime utility V. For example, suppose that w and z increase, but that v remains constant. Then V increases, given a positive probability to move residence, since the increase in commuting distance can be offset by moving residence.

In conclusion, we have derived the optimality conditions of individuals who search in the labour and housing market, whereas it also turned out to be possible to offer a sensible interpretation to these conditions.

The Optimal Strategy

The relationship between job mobility, residential mobility and commuting is certainly not easy to comprehend. For example, a current job move will affect future residential moving behaviour, whereas the expectation of a residence move will affect the current decision to move job. In order to increase understanding of the relationship between job mobility, residential mobility and commuting, we will analyse the optimal setting of res_w, the reservation wage set by an employed worker, and highlight the dependence on future job and residential moving behaviour.[9]

According to the search model proposed above, job and residential moving behaviour of an employed person are described by the transition rates. The transition rate of moving from the current job to another job $\theta_w(w,r,z)$ can be written as the product of the job offer arrival rate and the conditional probability of accepting a job offer. Similarly, the transition rate of moving residence $\theta_r(w,r,z)$ can be written as the product of the residential offer arrival rate and the conditional probability of accepting a residence offer:

$$\theta_w(w,r,z) = p_1 \int_0^{\bar{z}} \int_{res_w(y)}^{\bar{w}} d\,F_{wz}(x,y); \qquad \theta_r(w,r,z) = p_2 \int_0^{\bar{z}} \int_{res_r(y)}^{\bar{r}} d\,F_{rz}(x,y).$$

Hence the transition rate of moving job depends negatively on the reservation wage, whereas the transition rate of moving residence depends negatively on the reservation place utility. The optimal setting of the reservation wage in the current job depends on future job and residential moving behaviour. Therefore, we define the job and residential transition rates from a future position. We will focus on the transition rates in one of the minimum acceptable positions which may be obtained by a job move (the lifetime utility of this person after the move is equal to $V(res_w(z_y),r,z_y)$. The transition rate of moving job to another job can from this particular position be written as $\theta_w(res_w(z_y),r,z_y)$. Similarly, the transition rate of moving residence can then be written as $\theta_r(res_w(z_y),r,z_y)$. So

$$\theta_w\left(res_w(z_y),r,z_y\right)=p_1\int_0^{\bar{z}}\int_{res_w^2(y)}^{\bar{w}} dF_{wz}(x,y); \quad \theta_r\left(res_w(z_y),r,z_y\right)=p_2\int_0^{\bar{z}}\int_{res_r^w(y)}^{\bar{r}} dF_{rz}(x,y).$$

where we use the heretofore undefined indices $res_w^2(z_y)$ and $res_r^w(z_y)$. $res_w^2(z_y)$ is defined as the minimum wage which induces a second job move at the same distance z_y. Thus $res_w^2(z_y) = res_w(res_w(w,r,z|z_y),r,z_y|z_y)$. It can be easily shown that $res_w^2(z_y) > res_w(z_y)$ if $c_1 > 0$. $res_r^w(z_y)$ is defined as the minimum place utility which induces a *residential* move after the first job move at the same distance z_y. Thus $res_r^w(z_y) = res_r(res_w(w,r,z|z_y),r,z_y|z_y)$.

The optimal setting of the reservation wage res_w depends, among other things, on the functional form of the instantaneous utility function v. Interpretation of the optimal strategy is therefore facilitated by making assumptions about the functional form of the instantaneous utility function v. In this section we will suppose that v is a linear function in w, r and z, so $v(w,r,z) = w + \alpha.r - \beta.z$, where $\alpha, \beta > 0$. Thus the term $\beta.z$ can be interpreted as the commuting costs, and $w - \beta.z$ may be interpreted as the net wage, viz. the wage minus the commuting costs.

The optimal reservation wage strategy can now be rewritten as the sum of seven terms:

$$res_w(z_y) = w + \beta(z_y - z) + c_1[p + \gamma + \theta(res_w(z_y)r,z_y)]$$

$$+ p_2 \int_0^{\bar{z}} \int_{res_r^*(y)}^{res_r(y)} [V(res_w(z_y), x, y) - c_2 - V(res_w(z_y), r, z_y)] \, dF_{rz}(x, y)$$

$$- p_2 \int_0^{\bar{z}} \int_{res_r(y)}^{\bar{r}} [V(w, x, y) - V(res_w(z_y), x, y)] \, dF_{rz}(x, y)$$

(1)

$$+ p_2 \int_0^{\bar{z}} \int_{res_r(y)}^{\bar{r}} [V(w, x, y) - V(res_w(z_y), x, y)] \, dF_{rz}(x, y) + c_1 \theta_r (res_w(z_y), r, z_y).$$

Interpretation of the right hand side of (1) is facilitated by concentrating on a few special cases:

i) Suppose that the residential arrival rate is zero ($p_2 = 0$, and thus, $\theta_r = 0$), and that the costs of moving job are zero ($c_1 = 0$, and thus, $res_w = res_w^2$). This explains the first two terms on the right side of (1). The reservation wage can be written as $res_w(z_y) = w + \beta(z_y - z)$. This result makes sense. Given a job offer at a distance z_y, the job seeker demands at least the current wage plus the change in the commuting costs due to the job move. Whether the reservation wage is set higher or lower than the current wage depends on whether the commuting costs will increase or decrease. Not surprisingly, for this special case, the optimal reservation strategy can be rewritten as a function of the net wage: accept the job offer if $w_y - \beta.z_y > w - \beta.z$; otherwise, reject the job offer.

ii) Suppose that the rate of moving residence is zero ($p_2 = \theta_r = 0$), and the costs of moving job are positive ($c_1 > 0$). This case is a slight extension of a case thoroughly analysed by Hey and McKenna (1979) and Burgess (1992). Recall that persons take into account that after accepting a job offer, they may move job another time or leave the job involuntarily and that employed persons wish to be compensated for the moving costs. This explains the third term on the right side of (1). The amount of compensation depends on the time spent in the new job. So, $c_1.\rho$ can be interpreted as the long-run compensation and $c_1.[\theta_w(res_w(z_y), r, z_y) + \gamma]$ as the compensation for leaving the new job voluntarily or involuntarily (see also Van den Berg (1992). A well-known result in the literature is that the job seeker sets the reservation wage higher than would be necessary to be compensated for the job moving costs. This explains the fourth term. This term may be interpreted as 'to guard against the possibility of getting another wage offer after changing jobs that would have been preferred before changing, but which is not sufficiently high to induce a second change' (Hey and McKenna, 1979; Burgess, 1992).

iii) Finally, we will explain the last three terms on the right side of (1), and we suppose that the residential arrival rate is positive ($p_2 > 0$). The first of the last three terms in (1) is straightforward to interpret. After a job move, a worker may increase or decrease the reservation place utility. A change in the labour market may induce the worker to be less selective ($\text{res}_r^w(z_y) < \text{res}_r$), or to be more selective ($\text{res}_r^w(z_y) > \text{res}_r$), or to keep the residential strategy constant ($\text{res}_r^w(z_y) = \text{res}_r$). Consider the case when the worker is more selective after the job move ($\text{res}_r^w(z_y) > \text{res}_r$), and is therefore less likely to move residence after the job move. For this case, the term may be interpreted as the compensation required to guard against the possibility of getting a residential offer after changing jobs which would have been accepted if the job move had not occurred, but which is rejected after the job move. If the person will be less selective in the housing market and residential moves are more likely to occur, then this compensation will of course be negative. For example, a job move which leads to an increase in the commuting distance ($z_y > z$), and which will increase the likelihood of moving residence, will induce the person to lower the requested minimum wage.[10]

The penultimate term is the expected change in lifetime utility after a residential move due to change in the wage. This term is positive if $\text{res}_w < w$; otherwise it is non-positive. Finally, $c_1.\theta_r(\text{res}_w(z_y),r,z_y)$ can be interpreted as the amount required to compensate for the job moving costs due to a future residential move. Note that this term is invariably *positive* to compensate for the risk that a future residential move offsets the change in the commuting costs $\beta.(z_y-y)$. For example, this implies that workers may reject job offers that reduce the commuting distance, but which would have been accepted if the residential transition rate would have been zero. This implies that due to the existence of job moving costs and uncertainty about future residential moves, workers may commute more than they would otherwise do given the absence of such market imperfections.

Although we are able to interpret all the terms in (1), it is not easy to see how the spatial job acceptance region is affected by future job and residential moving behaviour. We will therefore approximate the above reservation strategy for a special case. Suppose that the wage offered equals the current wage.[11] As a result, every accepted job offer must then reduce the commuting distance (so $res_w = w$ and $z_y < z$, thus $res_r^w(z_y) > res_r$). Then we can determine z_{res}, which we define as the *maximum* commuting distance which would be accepted. For this special case, one can show that:

$$z_{res} \approx z - \phi c_1 [\rho + \gamma + \theta_w(w,r,z) + \theta_r(w,r,z_y)] - \tau [\theta_r(w,r,z) - \theta_r(w,r,z_y)] c_1$$

$$where \ \phi = \frac{1}{\beta} > 0 \ and \ \tau = \frac{\alpha}{\beta} > 0, \ 0 < \alpha < 1.$$

This result has a clear interpretation: workers accept only commuting distances shorter than the current commuting distance z. Workers nevertheless wish to be compensated for the investment of the moving costs and for the risk of moving job (voluntarily or involuntarily) or residence in the future. Furthermore, workers wish to be guarded against the possibility of getting a residential offer after changing jobs which would have been accepted if the job move would not have occurred.

Comparative Statics

The Wage, Place Utility, Commuting Distance, and Benefits

The optimal strategy depends on the current position of the individual in the labour and housing market. In Table 3.1, we show the results with respect to w, r, z and b. The results for the employed person are in line with intuition: the reservation wage is increasing in the wage and decreasing in the commuting distance, but the effect of the place utility on the reservation wage is undetermined. Similarly, the reservation place utility is increasing in the place utility and decreasing in the commuting distance, but the effect of the wage on the reservation place utility is undetermined. For those who are nonemployed however, the effects of changes in the characteristics on the optimal setting of the strategy are determined. A new result is that (i) the reservation place utility R_r is decreasing in the benefit b, and that (ii) the reservation wage R_w is increasing in r. An explanation for (i) is that those with higher benefits b are less inclined to accept a job, which increases the commuting distance. As a consequence, those with higher benefits are more likely to move residence after the job acceptance, which will induce them to move residence less often before the job acceptance (if $c_2 \geq 0$). An explanation for (ii) is that those with higher place utilities are more 'attached' to their present residential location, and are less willing to accept a job which induces a residential move. This result may be significant, as it makes clear that housing policies which discourage nonemployed persons to move residence (e.g. housing subsidies) will decrease the probability of becoming employed and may therefore unintentionally increase the number of nonemployed persons.

Table 3.1 Comparative Static Results
impact of changes in w, r, z and b on res_w, res_r, R_w and R_r.

	Employed			Nonemployed	
	res_w	res_r		R_w	R_r
Characteristic			Characteristic		
w	+	?	b	+	-
r	?	+	r	+	-
z	-	-			

+ = positive; - = negative ? = ambiguous   This table indicates, for example, that when a person is employed, the reservation wage res_w is increasing in the wage w, whereas it is decreasing in z.

Moving Costs, the Arrival Rates and the Firing Rate

Given the optimal strategy of individuals, it is also interesting to analyse the reactions of an individual given certain (comparative) exogenous changes in the environment. The results can be found in Table 3.2.

In the current paper, we are particularly interested in understanding the effect of changes in the housing market parameters (job market parameters) on job mobility (residential mobility). According to the model, when nonemployed, an increase in residential moving costs will induce a job searcher to be more selective in the labour market, which will result in a lower probability of accepting a job offer. The intuition behind this result is that when nonemployed, a job move then invariably leads to an increase in the commuting distance, and hence to a higher future probability of moving residence after the job move. As a result, an increase in the residential moving costs makes every job offer less attractive.

When employed however, the effect of an increase in residential moving costs has ambiguous effects on job mobility, since a job move may decrease or increase the commuting distance. Note that we are not able to determine the sign of p_2 on R_w, maybe in contrast to intuition. One might have expected that the residential arrival rate would decrease the reservation wage, as it would be more likely that the job seeker may reduce the commuting distance after the job acceptance. The explanation for this result seems to be that an increase in p_2 may sometimes reduce the residential hazard rate. Given plausible restrictions on the functional form of the place utility distribution however, it can be shown that the residential hazard will increase (see Van den Berg, 1994; for a contribution to this literature). We will not pursue this detail of the model any further.

Table 3.2 Comparative Static Results
impact of changes in c_1, c_2, γ, p_1 and p_2 on res_w, res_r, R_w and R_r.

parameter	Employed		Nonemployed	
	res_w	res_r	R_w	R_r
c_1	+	?	+	+
c_2	?	+	+	+
γ	+	?		
p_1	+	?	+	-?
p_2	?	+	-?	+

+ = positive; - = negative ? = ambiguous

As expected, an increase in the job moving costs c_1 decreases job mobility, but the effect on residential mobility is ambiguous due to two opposite effects. On the one hand, the probability to move residence will increase in order to compensate for the fact that there is a smaller probability that a job move reduces commuting distance. On the other hand, the probability to move residence will fall, because it is less likely that a residential move will increase commuting distance given a smaller probability that a job move will be used to decrease commuting distance.

A large number of transitions involves workers who are fired and become involuntarily nonemployed; whereas other (exogenous) transitions may involve workers who leave the labour market permanently (retirement, child rearing). Although the nonemployed period may be very short compared to the time spent employed, the effect on (costly) on-the-job mobility may be substantial (Burgess, 1992). One expects that the probability of becoming nonemployed γ will also affect residential mobility.

Facing a higher probability of becoming nonemployed, employed workers will voluntarily move job less frequently, as the once-only costs of moving have to be earned back within a shorter period (given $c_1 > 0$).[12] The effect of γ on residential mobility is ambiguous as an increase in the probability of becoming nonemployed has two opposite effects. For example, suppose that the current commuting distance is zero. Then after a residential move, commuting distance will increase. Given a higher probability of becoming nonemployed, the probability that the commuting distance will be decreased by a move into nonemployment is increased. As a result, moving residence becomes more attractive. Alternatively, suppose that the current commuting distance is large. Then there is less reason to move residence, because of a higher probability that the commuting distance will be decreased by a move into nonemployment.[13]

It might also be interesting to consider changes in the instantaneous utility function $v(w,r,z)$. Governments may, for example, deliberately increase the commuting costs by means of road pricing. Alternatively, congestion may increase the commuting costs. This implies that $|\partial v / \partial z|$ will increase. An exogenous increase in the general 'price' of commuting - so $|\partial v / \partial z|$ increases - will affect the job and residence acceptance behaviour of employed and nonemployed persons. A formal proof is unnecessary to see that the effect of an increase in the general price of commuting on moving behaviour of employed persons is ambiguous. For example, if the current commuting distance is zero, the probability to move job or residence declines if the price goes up, since every alternative is less attractive. Alternatively, if commuting distance obtains its maximum value, an increase in the price of commuting will always increase job and residential mobility. Furthermore, it is clear that an increase in the price of commuting will induce nonemployed persons to be more selective in the labour market, because every job alternative is less attractive. Finally, the effect on residential moving behaviour is ambiguous.[14]

In conclusion, one of the main conclusions drawn from the comparative static effects for *employed* persons as reported in Table 3.2 is that the effect of the labour market parameters (c_1, p_1 and γ) on res_w are all determined, but the effect on the housing market variables (c_2 and p_2) are in general ambiguous. Similarly, the effect of the housing market parameters (c_2 and p_2) on res_r are all determined, but the effect on the labour market variables (c_1, p_2 and γ) are ambiguous. This somewhat disappointing result is, of course, the result of the generality of the model proposed, as we do not make any assumption on the ordering of the job and housing offers. Fortunately, unambiguous results can be obtained for some special cases (see next section). In contrast to the ambiguous result for the effect of the residential moving costs c_2 on the acceptance behaviour for the employed, the effect on the acceptance behaviour for the *nonemployed* is determined. Nonemployed persons accept fewer jobs if the residential moving costs are higher, because it is more costly to reduce the commuting distance after the job move.

Although the effect of the job moving costs on the residential hazard rate, and the effect of the residential moving costs on the job hazard rate are ambiguous, the effect of an increase in these costs on the sum of the job and residential hazard rate are determined:

$$\partial(\theta_w(w,r,z) + \theta_r(w,r,z)/\partial c_1 \geq 0;$$
$$\partial(\theta_w(w,r,z) + \theta_r(w,r,z)/\partial c_2 \geq 0.$$

The effect of an increase in the job moving costs on the sum of the job and residential hazard rates is negative; an increase in the residential moving costs also decreases the sum of the job and residential hazard rates. This result has a straightforward interpretation. For example, the effect on an increase in the residential moving costs on the job hazard rate is less than the (absolute) effect on the residential hazard rate (so, $\partial\theta_w/\partial c_2 < |\partial\theta_r/\partial c_2|$). This result is due to the fact that the job hazard rate is affected by an increase in c_2, because the residence hazard rate is affected by an increase in c_2. This result will be useful in the next section.

Moving Costs; Three Special Cases

In Table 3.2 we found that the sign of the residential moving costs c_2 on the reservation wage of an employed person res_w is ambiguous. In this section we will show that in certain cases this sign can be determined. We will discuss some of these cases here.

i)   the wage distribution is degenerated; this is common in labour markets which are highly institutionalised and where wage differences are minimal.

ii) the current commuting distance is zero; many workers are close to this situation. For example, in the Netherlands, about 50% percent of all workers commute for less than 15 minutes and less than 10 kilometres (EBB, 1992). In other European countries (United Kingdom, France, Austria, Sweden) workers commute even less (Jansen, 1992).

iii) the residence hazard rate is zero, whereas it may become positive after a job move. This case is relevant for persons who do not plan to move residence due to the high moving costs, but who still expect to make a labour market move. Such a labour market move may increase the commuting distance which gives an incentive to move residence after the job move.

i)   Suppose that jobs are homogeneous such that the wage distribution is degenerated. Thus, jobs only differ with respect to their location. Then it can be shown that the reservation wage res_w is non-increasing in c_2, so the job hazard rate is non-decreasing in c_2.[15] The interpretation is straightforward. When jobs are homogeneous then job movements occur only in order to reduce the commuting distance. If residential moving costs c_2 are higher, then it will be relatively less costly to decrease the commuting distance by moving job than by moving residence.[16]

ii)   Suppose that the current commuting distance z is zero. It can be shown that $\partial res_w(w,r,0|z_y)/\partial c_2 \geq 0$. This result has the following interpretation. Any job move will increase the commuting distance. If c_2 is higher, then it will be less likely that the commuting distance will be reduced by moving residence, so this discourages accepting a job offer now.

iii)   When the residential hazard rate is currently zero, then an increase in c_2 decreases the job hazard rate (increases res_w). This result is due to the fact that after a certain job move which may increase the commuting distance, the probability of moving residence may become positive. As a consequence, the search model predicts that in economies in which (very) high residential moving costs are prevalent, it is likely that a (further) increase in the moving costs will induce persons to move job less often.

We conclude that the uncertainty in Table 3.2 on the sign of the residential moving costs c_2 on the reservation wage of an employed person res_w can be removed in specific cases.

If the current commuting distance z is (close to) zero or if the residential moving costs are (very) high then job mobility depends negatively on the residential moving costs c_2; if the wage distribution is degenerated, then job mobility depends positively on the residential moving costs c_2. A similar approach can of course be used to investigate the other uncertainties in Tables 3.1 and 3.2.

Do Workers First Move Job, and Then Move Residence?

In the expressions derived above, the search model appears symmetric, which is counter-intuitive, because it is observed that, in *general*, workers will first accept a new job and then search for a new residence; see, for example, Verster (1986) and Camstra (1993). This issue may be solved by focusing on the parameters of the search process on both markets. Consider the case when the ratio of residence and job offers p_2/p_1 is likely to be large, because finding a job is, in general, far more difficult than finding another residence. Given the values of these parameters, the search model is consistent with the observation that after a job move which increases the commuting distance, an individual would almost immediately move residence as the probability of a residence offer is high. After a residence move which increases the commuting distance, it may take considerable time before a worker will adjust the workplace location (as p_1 is low). This case seems to be the most common situation (in developed countries). However, under particular circumstances the opposite may be found for certain subgroups, thus p_2/p_1 is small. For example, the typical low income employee in the Netherlands rents a subsidised residence in a market which is highly regulated, with a small probability that a residence offer will arrive. Our model would then predict that this worker is inclined to refuse job offers which are farther from his current residence; this typical low income employee would likely be more willing to move residence (given an offer) even if this implies that commuting distance is increased. In sum, the model indicates that workers generally accept first a new job and then move residence closer to the new workplace location. This sequence may be reversed, depending on the conditions on the labour and housing market.

Conclusion

We have derived a search model that aims to explain on-the-job and residential relocation behaviour of employed individuals. An essential feature of the model is that workers who consider a job or residential move take into account future residential and job moving behaviour. The model includes commuting distance, which alters after every residential and job move. The optimal strategy is derived and interpreted. Comparative statics results are derived. One of main conclusions based upon the search model is that the effect of factors which cause housing market imperfections (viz. the residential moving costs and the residence arrival rate) have ambiguous effects on the job acceptance and job search behaviour of employed individuals. For some interesting cases however, the effect of the residential moving costs on the job acceptance behaviour is unambiguous. Particularly, if the current commuting distance is zero, then job mobility depends non-positively on residential moving costs; if the wage distribution is degenerated, then job mobility depends non-negatively on residential moving costs. Those persons who are nonemployed however, will accept fewer job offers and search less intensively in the labour market when residential moving costs are higher. As a result, housing policies which discourage nonemployed persons to move residence (e.g. housing subsidies) also decrease the probability of becoming employed and may therefore unintentionally increase the number of nonemployed persons. Finally, the model is consistent with the stylised fact that employed persons generally accept new jobs first and then move their residence closer to the new work location, although it is explained that this sequence depends on the specific labour and housing market conditions.

Notes

[1] The same holds true for theories which explain the job and residential mobility after a relocation of the workplace; see Zax and Kain (1991) or Van Wee (1993).

[2] We are only concerned with full-time employed workers; therefore the costs concomitant with a job, such as the loss of leisure, which are equal for all job alternatives, can be ignored.

[3] Of course, for some particular professions (e.g. clergymen), the job and dwelling offers are strongly dependent, but these are not common.

[4] For example, because reimbursement of travelling expenses, which is distance-dependent, is often (positively) related to the wage level. In the Netherlands, the income tax depends negatively on the commuting distance.

[5] More realistic assumptions would be to allow for time-varying exogenous changes in the place utility (for example due to changes in the household composition) and to allow for endogenous changes in the place utility due to changes in the wage (i.e. the demand for housing depends on income). See, for example, Linneman and Graves (1983).

[6] See Burgess (1992) for the effect of the costs of becoming re-employed.

[7] Hence, it is noted that a study of acceptance behaviour given a simultaneous job and a residence offer is not possible within our framework. Such a framework would allow for pooling of job and residential offers for a certain period. Such an extension is beyond the aim of this paper.

[8] The decision rules are arbitrary in the sense that these do not maximise V and U.

[9] The analyses of R_w, res_r and R_r are similar, and will therefore not be discussed in detail.

[10] It is noteworthy that there exist several reasons why individuals accept jobs with a lower wage than the wage currently earned (e.g., better working conditions, more job security). As an additional reason our model indicates that employed individuals may accept some job offers with a lower net wage - the wage minus the commuting costs - because the commuting distance can be reduced by a residential move.

[11] This may be relevant if the wage distribution is degenerated. This may particularly occur in labour markets which are highly institutionalised, and where the variations in the wages are very small.

[12] Notice that if the probability of becoming nonemployed is firm-specific, one expects the opposite result.

[13] In general however, one expects that the second effect will often be important, such that workers facing a higher probability of becoming employed will refuse jobs, because it is too risky to reduce commuting distance with a residence move.

[14] On one hand, it is less likely that a job move occurs, so the probability of moving residence in the future is reduced. It is now less 'risky' to move residence. On the other hand, if a job move occurs, the probability of moving residence is increased, so it is now more risky to move residence.

[15] To be more precise, res_w is non-increasing in c_2. If z is equal to 0, then an increase in z will have no effect on res_w.

[16] Note that if jobs are heterogeneous, then an increase in c_2 may induce the worker to accept fewer jobs from a long commuting distance.

4. Moving Behaviour of Two-Earner Households

Introduction

This chapter focuses on the relationship between residential and job moving decisions and commuting behaviour for two-earner households.[1] The case of two-earner households deserves special attention because the two wage earners in the same household share a dwelling, but have separate working places. Having separate places of employment adds to the complexity of their spatial decision problem. The practical importance of this topic is evident from the currently high number of wage earners who form a two-earner household, and it is still growing, mainly because of increased participation of women in the labour market. Nevertheless, in general, not much is known about the moving and commuting behaviour for two-earner households both theoretically and empirically. The few available theoretical studies of commuting behaviour for two-earner households are mainly based on static urban equilibrium models (see, for example, White, 1977, 1986; Madden, 1981). Moreover, empirical studies of commuting behaviour for two-earner households are often interpreted by means of static models (see Madden, 1981; Curran et al, 1982; White, 1977, 1988; Singell and Lillydahl, 1986 and Dubin, 1991). Static models typically ignore the effect of future residential and job moves on the choice of the present commuting distance.[2] In this chapter, we will address the above issue and focus explicitly on the consequences of future moves by making use of search theory.

We introduce a search model which extends the usual search models in several ways. First, we acknowledge that workers take into account commuting distance in their decision-making; second, we allow for job and residential moving costs; and third, the households consist of two wage earners. In this case, non-trivial results are obtained. We will make clear that the decision to move is not only affected by the commuting distance of the other wage earner in the same household, but is also affected by the distance between the workplaces of the two wage earners in the same household.

Specifically, both wage earners have higher job mobility rates if the distance between the workplaces is larger. Though it appears to be difficult to compare moving and commuting behaviour for two-earner households and single wage-earners, the search model clearly indicates that in most cases, two-earner households will have lower job mobility rates than single wage-earners.

The chapter is organised as follows. First, a search model is developed which analyses residential and job moving behaviour for two-earner households. Then we derive some comparative statics of the search model. Next, we discuss the potential effect of divorce for the outcomes of the model and we compare the behaviour of single wage-earners and two-earner households. Finally, we offer a concluding section.

The Search Model

The Model Specification

Search theory generally aims to explain the behaviour of individuals who search for jobs or residences in order to improve their current situation (for a review, see Mortensen, 1986 or Devine and Kiefer, 1993). In this chapter, we concentrate on the behaviour of two-earner households who search simultaneously for better jobs and residences (see Chapter 3 for an analysis of one-earner households). We suppose that the household consists of two wage earners who currently earn wages w_1 and w_2 respectively.[3] The present residence renders a place utility of value r. The commuting distances due to the travel between the current workplaces and the residence are denoted by z_1 and z_2. The instantaneous utility v experienced in a certain period by the household is a function of w_1, z_1, w_2, z_2 and r. So, $v = v(w_1, z_1, w_2, z_2, r)$. We assume that $\partial v / \partial w_i > 0$, $\partial v / \partial z_i < 0$, $i=1,2$, and $\partial v / \partial r > 0$. Hence, instantaneous utility increases in wages and place utility, and decreases in commuting distance. These assumptions allow for a wide range of particular forms of the instantaneous utility v.[4]

It should be noted that virtually all search models in the current literature are based upon the assumption that the decision unit consists of one individual. The two wage earners of a two-earner household share a dwelling but have different working places so the spatial residential behaviour affects the spatial job behaviour of both wage earners. In the sequel, we will demonstrate that this implies that the distance between the workplace locations of the wage earners, which is denoted by z_3, affects the residential and job moving behaviour of both wage earners. In Figure 4.1 we have drawn the relationship between z_1, z_2 and z_3.

Figure 4.1 The Workplace and Residential Locations of Two-Earner Household

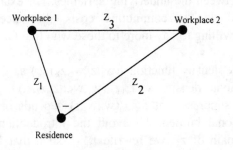

In many theoretical and empirical job and residential moving studies, the importance of moving costs as a factor that reduces mobility is emphasised (see, inter alia, Zax, 1991, 1994; Boehm, 1981, Ioannides, 1987; Van den Berg, 1992; Hugh and McCormick, 1985; Hey and McKenna, 1979). In line with these studies, we assume that moving job and moving dwelling is costly. Residential moving costs are denoted by c_h, and job moving costs are denoted by c_1 and c_2, respectively. For convenience of notation, we suppose that the instantaneous utility v is a standardised linear function of the job and residential moving costs. Thus, we suppose that $v(c_1 + \delta_1, c_2 + \delta_2, c_h + \delta_3)$ - $v(c_1, c_2, c_h) = -\delta_1 - \delta_2 - \delta_3$.[5] In the basic version of the search model, search is costless so wage earners search continuously for new jobs and dwellings. The search process will result in job or residential offers which arrive randomly. We define the period in our model by requiring that the probability of getting two or more offers in any period is negligible. At most, one offer is received each period: wage earner 1 receives job offers with probability p_1, wage earner 2 receives job offers with probability p_2, and residence offers arrive with probability p_3. Of course, $p_1 + p_2 + p_3 < 1$. Every time a residence or job offer arrives, the household decides instantaneously whether or not to accept the job or residence offer. It is supposed that the household maximises expected lifetime utility in a stationary environment. Expected lifetime utility is denoted as V.

We assume that every job or residence offer is a random drawing from a continuous joint density $f(w_1,z_1,w_2,z_2,r,z_3)$.[6] Wage earner 1 receives job offers from $f(w_1,z_1,z_3)$, wage earner 2 receives job offers from $f(w_2,z_2,z_3)$, and the two-earner households receive residential offers from $f(z_1,z_2,r)$. The corresponding cumulative distribution function is denoted by F. In the notation we suppress that the density f is conditional on exogenous characteristics.[7] It should be noted that we allow all kinds of interdependencies between the underlying variables. For example, w_1 and z_1 might be correlated due to commuting costs allowances, or because employers might be willing to pay more to those who live far from the job at the time of hiring.

We rewrite the density function $f(w_1,z_1,w_2,z_2,r,z_3)$ as the product of a marginal and conditional density, so $f_{w1,w2,r}(w_1,w_2,r|z_1,z_2,z_3).f_{z1,z2,z3}(z_1,z_2,z_3)$. In the sequel, we will suppress that $f_{w1,w2,r}(w_1,w_2,r)$ depends on z_1,z_2,z_3 which decreases the notational burden. To avoid the introduction of additional notation for the domain of z_3,[8] we rewrite $f_{z1,z2,z3}$ such that $f_{z1,z2,z3}$ exists on $[0,\infty)x[0,\infty)x[0,\infty)$, so $f_{z1,z2,z3}$ is zero outside the original domain of z_3.

The aim of this chapter is to understand the spatial moving behaviour of two-earner households. Note that a residential move does not alter the distance between the workplaces. The two-earner household will search for new residences and evaluate the residence offered, *conditional on the current value of z_3*. Hence, the functional form of $f_{z1,z2}(z_1,z_2|z_3)$ determines the spatial behaviour for two-earner households. $f_{z1,z2}(z_1,z_2|z_3)$ is not an arbitrary joint density function, since z_1, z_2 and z_3 form a triangle. For example, given an increase in z_3, it will be more likely that the offer of either z_1 or z_2 will be larger. A property of the joint density $f_{z1,z2,z3}(z_1,z_2,z_3)$ is that

$$\frac{\partial F_{z_1,z_2}(z_1,z_2|z_3)}{\partial z_3}<0$$

which states that a marginal increase in z_3 decreases the probability of obtaining an offer less than z_1 and less than z_2. In other words, the joint distribution of z_1 and z_2 is stochastically increasing in z_3. Furthermore, note that a job move by one wage earner does not alter the commuting distance of the other wage earner, so job offers are evaluated conditional on the commuting distance of the other wage earner.[9]

The Construction of the Lifetime Utility and the Optimality Conditions

In our analysis we assume that two-earner households maximise expected lifetime utility, hence job and residence offers will be accepted (or rejected) depending on whether or not these offers will increase lifetime utility. The lifetime utility depends on the current wages and commuting distances of both wage earners, the place utility of the dwelling and the distance between the workplaces, so $V = V(w_1,z_1,w_2,z_2,r,z_3)$. The lifetime utility can be written as the sum of the instantaneous utility and the expected benefit of accepting a residential or job offer discounted at rate ρ. $V(w_1,z_1,w_2,z_2,r,z_3)$ can be written as:

$$V(w_1,z_1,w_2,z_2,r,z_3) = v(w_1,z_1,w_2,z_2,r) + \rho V(w_1,z_1,w_2,z_2,r,z_3)$$

$$+ p_1 \rho \int_0^\infty \int_0^\infty \int_0^\infty \max[0,V(x_1,y_1,w_2,z_2,r,y_3) - c_1 - V(w_1,z_1,w_2,z_2,r,z_3)] f_{z_{1,z_3}}(y_1,y_3|z_2) f_{w_1}(x_1) dy_3 dx_1 dy_1$$

$$+ p_2 \rho \int_0^\infty \int_0^\infty \int_0^\infty \max[0,V(w_1,z_1,x_2,y_2,r,y_3) - c_2 - V(w_1,z_1,w_2,z_2,r,z_3)] f_{z_{2,z_3}}(y_2,y_3|z_1) f_{w_2}(x_2) dy_3 dx_2 dy_2$$

$$+ p_3 \rho \int_0^\infty \int_0^\infty \int_0^\infty \max[0,V(w_1,y_1,w_2,y_2,h,z_3) - c_h - V(w_1,z_1,w_2,z_2,r,z_3)] f_{z_{1,z_2}}(y_1,y_2|z_3) f_r(h) dh dy_1 dy_2$$

The right-hand side of this equation can easily be explained. The first term equals the utility received in the present period. In the next period, if the household neither moves residence nor job, then it will have a lifetime utility $V(w_1,z_1,w_2,z_2,r,z_3)$, discounted at rate ρ. The third term equals the change in lifetime utility due to a job move by wage earner 1. The job will only be accepted given an increase in lifetime utility, taking into account moving costs c_1. It is important to note that we acknowledge that the distribution of z_1, z_3 depends on z_2. The last two terms can be explained in a similar way.

Let us now focus on the role which z_3 plays in the lifetime utility V, as the distance between the workplaces does explicitly appear in our model, whereas it is absent in other search models which concentrate on search behaviour in one market. We suppose that z_3 does not affect instantaneous utility. Nevertheless, it influences lifetime utility since it influences the expected benefit of moving residence, and hence also the expected benefit of moving job. As a consequence, if the household would never move in the housing market (e.g. $p_3 = 0$), then V and job mobility do not depend on z_3.

The basic decision the household has to take is whether to accept a job or residence offer, taking into account other offers in the future. For most search models, the optimal strategy implies that the household follows a decision rule. For example, in virtually all known on-the-job search models, reservation wage rules exist which read as follows: given a wage offer w_x: change job if $v(w_x) > res_w(v(w))$, otherwise do not change job, where res_w is called the reservation wage (to distinguish between the current characteristics and the characteristics offered, we add a subscript 'x' to the characteristics offered). For example, w_{1x} denotes the wage offered to wage earner 1. An important difference between our model and these search models is that we acknowledge that behaviour in one of the markets affects behaviour in another market. If workers search in different markets, this simple type of reservation wage rule generally does in general not exist. For example, one can see that the decision rule: change job if $v(w_{1x},z_{1x},w_{2x},z_{2x},r) > res_w(v(w_1,z_1,w_2,z_2,r))$, otherwise do not change job, is *not* consistent: the decision rule does not acknowledge that different combinations of w_1, z_1, w_2, z_2, and r which render the same value of v must lead to different job moving decisions.[10] We follow another route by constructing reservation rules which do not depend on the instantaneous utility function v, but which directly depend on all current characteristics w_1, z_1, w_2, z_2, r and z_3.

Decision rules Given a job offer to wage earner i (i =1,2) of wage w_{ix}, commuting distances z_{ix} and distance z_{3x}, and given w_1,z_1,w_2,z_2,r,z_3 and *reservation wage* $res_{wi}(w_1,z_1,w_2,z_2,r,z_3|z_{ix},z_{3x})$:

change job   if $w_{ix} > res_{wi}(w_1,z_1,w_2,z_2,r,z_3|z_{ix},z_{3x})$, i =1,2;
                    otherwise, do not change job.

Given a residential *offer* of place utility r_x and commuting distances z_{1x} and z_{2x}, and given w_1,z_1,w_2,z_2,r,z_3 and *reservation place utility* $res_r(w_1,z_1,w_2,z_2,r,z_3|z_{1x},z_{2x})$:

change residence if $r_x > res_r(w_1,z_1,w_2,z_2,r,z_3|z_{1x},z_{2x})$;
                     otherwise, do not change residence.

To simplify the notation, we will suppress that the reservation wage and reservation place utility depend on the current position and we will use $res_{wi}(z_{ix},z_{3x})$, i=1,2 and $res_r(z_{1x},z_{2x})$. Moreover, in the case that it is of no interest to emphasise that these reservation indices depend on particular values of z_{ix}, i=1,2,3, we use res_{w1}, res_{w2} and res_r.

These decision rules define the dynamic maximisation problem, because the household maximises the lifetime utility by choosing optimal values for res_{w1}, res_{w2} and res_r. These optimal values can be calculated using the first-order conditions. These first-order conditions can be rewritten as:

$$V(w_1,z_{1x},w_2,z_{2x},res_r(z_{1x},z_{2x}),z_3) = V(w_1,z_1,w_2,z_2,r,z_3) + c_h \qquad (a)$$

$$V(res_{w1}(z_{1x},z_{3x}),z_{1x},w_2,z_2,r,z_{3x}) = V(w_1,z_1,w_2,z_2,r,z_3) + c_1 \qquad (b)$$

$$V(w_1,z_1,res_{w2}(z_{2x},z_{3x}),z_{2x},r,z_{3x}) = V(w_1,z_1,w_2,z_2,r,z_3) + c_2 \qquad (c)$$

The above formulae have straightforward interpretations. For example, the first-order condition (a) has the following interpretation: given a commuting distance offer of value z_{1x} and z_{2x}, and given a place utility offer of value $res_r(z_{1x},z_{2x})$, the household is indifferent between moving residence and not moving residence. As moving residence is costly, the lifetime value of the utility associated with the reservation place utility is equal to the sum of the present value of the lifetime utility plus the cost of moving residence. The first-order conditions (b) and (c) offer similar interpretations.

To understand the spatial moving behaviour of two-earner households, it is necessary to know how the characteristics (w_1, z_1, w_2, z_2, r and z_3) affect lifetime utility and the reservation rules. Hence, in the sequel we will focus on the effects of changes in the characteristics on lifetime utility, the optimal decision rules and moving behaviour.

Comparative Statics

Comparative Statics: Lifetime Utility

The effects of changes in z_1, z_2 and z_3 on lifetime utility are derived in Van Ommeren, Rietveld and Nijkamp (1997). It can be shown that:

$$(i) \frac{\partial V(w_1,z_1,w_2,z_2,r,z_3)}{\partial z_1} < 0; \quad (ii) \frac{\partial V(w_1,z_1,w_2,z_2,r,z_3)}{\partial z_2} < 0; \quad (iii) \frac{\partial V(w_1,z_1,w_2,z_2,r,z_3)}{\partial z_3} \leq 0$$

These results make sense. (*i*) and (*ii*) imply that an increase in the current commuting distances z_1 or z_2 reduces lifetime utility V. This is, of course, the consequence of the fact that an increase in one of the current commuting distances reduces the value of the current instantaneous utility v. A novelty of the model presented is (*iii*). It states that the lifetime utility decreases as the distance between the workplaces z_3 increases. As z_3 does not affect instantaneous utility v, we interpret this result as follows: given an increase in z_3, the probability of receiving a residential offer with large values for z_1 and z_2 increases. As z_1 and z_2 are a cost to the household, lifetime utility $V(w_1, z_1, w_2, z_2, r, z_3)$ decreases as the expected benefit of moving residence is reduced. z_3 has no effect on lifetime utility only if the probability of moving residence is zero.

The effects of other characteristics on lifetime utility are the following: $\partial V/\partial w_1 > 0$, $\partial V/\partial w_2 > 0$ and $\partial V/\partial r > 0$. An increase in the wage or in place utility therefore increases lifetime utility. These results are summarised in Table 4.1.

Comparative Statics: The Reservation Rules

Changes in the current characteristics affect lifetime utility V. One expects that these changes will affect the decision rules which determine whether or not to accept a residence or job offer. First, we will focus on the effect on the reservation place utility. It can be shown that:

$$(i) \ \partial res_r/\partial z_1 < 0; \quad \partial res_r/\partial z_2 < 0$$

It is clear that (i) implies that reservation place utility decreases due to an increase in commuting distances z_1 or z_2. The implication of this result is that when the commuting distance of one wage earner is larger, the household will be less choosy with respect to residence offers. In other words, given an increase in commuting distance, more residential offers will be accepted.

Furthermore, it has been shown that:

$$(ii) \ \partial res_r/\partial z_3 \leq 0$$

This implies that reservation place utility decreases due to an increase in the distance between the workplaces z_3. One may interpret this as follows. Given an increase in z_3, the household will receive dwelling offers which imply larger values for z_1 and z_2. As shown above, an increase in z_3 reduces the household's lifetime utility. From a deteriorated position, there exist more job-residence combinations which improve the position. Therefore, the household will be less choosy and will accept *more* residence offers (so res_r falls). It is important to notice that this does *not* imply that residential mobility also increases given an increase in z_3, because the distribution of commuting offers $f_{z1,z2}$ is also affected by an increase in z_3, which also affects residential mobility. In fact, we will make clear later on that even if households are less choosy, they may move residence less often.

The effects of an increase in z_1, z_2 or z_3 on the reservation wages are as follows:

$$(i) \quad \partial \text{res}_{w1}/\partial z_1 < 0; \quad \partial \text{res}_{w2}/\partial z_2 < 0;$$

$$(ii) \quad \partial \text{res}_{w1}/\partial z_3 \leq 0; \quad \partial \text{res}_{w2}/\partial z_3 \leq 0;$$

$$(iii) \quad \partial \text{res}_{w1}/\partial z_2 = ?; \quad \partial \text{res}_{w2}/\partial z_1 = ?;$$

In line with intuition, (*i*) implies that the reservation wage of a wage earner decreases due to an increase in his/her commuting distance. The implication of this result is that given an increase in the commuting distance, wage earners are less choosy with respect to job offers. According to (*ii*), the reservation wage decreases in z_3, so both wage earners will accept more job offers. The explanation for this effect is as follows: given an increase in z_3, lifetime utility decreases, because z_3 decreases the probability of obtaining a residence offer with low values for z_1 and z_2. This gives the household an incentive to *reduce* z_3 via a job move in order that the probability of obtaining a *future* residential offer with low values for z_1 and z_2 is increased. Hence, an increase in the distance between the workplace locations makes other jobs more attractive (so res_{w1} and res_{w2} fall).

Result (*iii*) implies that the effect of an increase in the commuting distance of one wage earner has an ambiguous effect on the reservation wage of the spouse. This result for $\partial \text{res}_{w1}/\partial z_2$ might be explained as follows: given an increase in z_2, the household will be more likely to move residence. As a consequence, it is less 'worthwhile' for wage earner 1 to accept jobs closer to the current residential location, but it is more 'worthwhile' for individual 1 to accept jobs which are far from the current residential location. As a result, the sign of $\partial \text{res}_{w1}/\partial z_2$ is ambiguous. A similar reasoning holds for $\partial \text{res}_{w2}/\partial z_1$.

The effects of other characteristics are the following: the reservation wage depends positively on his/her current wage ($\partial \text{res}_{w1}/\partial w_1 > 0$, $\partial \text{res}_{w2}/\partial z_2 > 0$). Moreover, the reservation place utility increases as the current place utility increases ($\partial \text{res}_r/\partial r > 0$). These results are summarised in Table 4.1.

Comparative Statics: Job and Residential Moving Behaviour

Given the results of the effect of a change in the current characteristics on the reservation place utility and the reservation wages, one may determine the effect of a change in the current characteristics on the job and residential mobility rates. If the probability of receiving an offer in a period of length h is approximately equal to $p_i.h$, then we may interpret p_i as an arrival rate (i =1,2,3), and we may make use of the concept of the transition rate - also called the hazard rate[11] - which is easy to estimate given information on durations. The hazard rate for voluntarily leaving the present job is defined as the product of the job offer arrival rate and the conditional probability of accepting a job offer. The hazard rate for moving residence is defined as the product of the residence offer arrival rate and the conditional probability of accepting a residence offer. We denote the hazard rates for moving job as θ_{w1} and θ_{w2}. We denote the hazard rate for moving residence as θ_r.

Table 4.1 Comparative Static Results

Characteristic	V	res_{w1}	res_{w2}	res_r	θ_{w1}	θ_{w2}	θ_r
z_1	-	-	?	-	+	?	+
z_2	-	?	-	-	?	+	+
z_3	-	-	-	-	+	+	?
w_1	+	+	?	?	-	?	?
w_2	+	?	+	?	?	-	?
r	+	+	+	+	?	?	-

+ = positive; - = negative; ? = ambiguous

In Table 4.1 the effects of the characteristics on lifetime utility, the reservation indices and the hazard rates are summarised. Interpretation of the impacts on the hazard rates is straightforward and intuitively easy to understand, given the results derived above. For example, we have found that both wage earners are more willing to move job if the distance between the workplaces of the two wage earners in the same household is higher ($\partial res_{wi}/\partial z_3 < 0$, i=1,2). This explains why both wage earners are more likely to move job ($\partial\theta_{wi}/\partial z_3 > 0$, i=1,2).[12] Finally, the comparative static results obtained for moving behaviour of single-wage earners with respect to the wage, place utility and commuting distance (see Chapter 3) are identical to the results obtained here for the moving behaviour of members of two-earner households.

Divorce

The search model discussed above is very stylised and is not in all respects very realistic. We have assumed that the household consists of two wage earners who live together forever in the same household. Since many couples break their relationship, this may affect job and residential behaviour of two-earner households. For example, residential relocations which are beneficial to the household may have a negative effect on the lifetime utility of one wage earner, if he/she will divorce. An extension of the model which allows for divorce may be analysed with game-theoretic tools as both wage earners have conflicting interests. Such a model will not be discussed here. Alternatively, given the reasonable assumption that both wage earners wish to avoid any signal which shows that they take into account that they expect a divorce in the near future, two-earner households will behave according to the search model proposed here.

A Comparison of Behaviour of Two-Earners and Single Wage-Earner Households

A formal comparison of moving behaviour of two-earner households and single wage-earners based on the search model is not straightforward, because the decision process of single wage-earners and two-earner households is structurally different, but some insights can be obtained based on search theory. The following distinction between two types of single wage-earner households might be helpful.

Type 1: The household consists of an employed (number 1) and an nonemployed spouse (number 2) who both search in the labour market. The instantaneous monetary utility derived from being nonemployed equals w_2.[13]

Type 2: The household consists of only one employed person (actually, this person may have a nonemployed spouse who is not available for the labour market).

The obvious difference between these two types of households is that the expected job career of a non-employed spouse affects the lifetime utility of the household, and accordingly the behaviour of the employed spouse. One may then conjecture that an employed person with an nonemployed spouse would generally be more reluctant to accept large commuting costs z_1 than those persons without a spouse (recall that z_1 stochastically increases z_2 and z_3). When the nonemployed spouse becomes employed then it will be more costly for the two-earner household to decrease the commuting distances.

Of more direct empirical relevance would more likely be the impact the employed spouse has on the behaviour of a non-employed spouse. This impact is much stronger, because the nonemployed spouse searches conditional on the current position of the employed spouse. The conjectured asymmetry in behaviour between an employed and nonemployed spouse may add to the observed differences in labour market behaviour between men and women.[14] When the nonemployed spouse becomes employed then the increase in lifetime utility might be substantially less than if the nonemployed person would be alone (because z_2 and z_3 become positive, which both reduce lifetime utility). We conjecture that nonemployed workers who have an employed spouse set higher reservation wages and are therefore less likely to accept a job offer from a large distance than those without an employed spouse. Thus, nonemployed workers with an employed spouse may be much more selective with respect to jobs from a large distance than those who are alone.

A comparison between two-earner households and single wage-earners renders the following conclusion. First of all, examples can be given which show that two-earner households may move more or may move less than single wage-earners depending on the situation Two-earner households are less prone to move residence than single wage-earners given very short commuting distances (and a short distance between the workplaces), and they are more likely to move residence given large commuting distances and short distance between the workplaces.

Although unambiguous results cannot be obtained with respect to moving behaviour, we will clarify that, in general, two-earner households will more often reject job offers which would be accepted by single wage-earners. Suppose that employment is uniformly distributed over space (see also Rouwendal and Rietveld, 1994):

$$f(z) = \begin{cases} c.2.\pi.z & \text{for } z < z_{max} \\ 0 & \text{elsewhere} \end{cases}$$

where c denotes a normalisation constant and z_{max} is the maximum value of z. The expected value of the commuting distance offered is $2/3.z_{max}$. Let us consider a wage earner of whom the *current* commuting distance is 1/5 of the maximum of the commuting distances offered.[15] The probability that a job offer will reduce the current commuting distance equals 0.04, so the probability that a job offer will increase the commuting distance equals 0.96. More examples may certainly be listed but one may safely conclude that in general, the probability of receiving an attractive job offer (in terms of wages) on a large commuting distance is much higher than receiving an attractive offer nearby. Let us suppose that a single wage-earner from type 1 and a wage-earner who has an employed spouse receive a job offer which increases the commuting distance. If the household reduces the commuting distance of the job offered via a residential move, the commuting distance of the other wage earner most probably increase.

Intuitively, it may seem that two-earner households will have longer commutes than single wage-earners, because if two wage earners share a dwelling they have fewer opportunities to reduce commuting distances via a residential move. Notice however that this intuition is not formally supported by search theory. Although single wage-earners are better able to reach a more favourable situation, they will more often accept long commutes for short periods (as they may reduce the commuting distance more easily). Thus we arrive at an ambiguous conclusion concerning the impact of household type on commuting distances. Such a result, based on a theoretical dynamic model, is also found in Curran et al (1982) who base their analysis on a static equilibrium model of residential location in separate urban employment centres. In addition empirical investigations of single wage-earners and two-earner households do not render conclusive results on this topic (see, among others, White, 1986 or Madden, 1981 for the U.S. or Rouwendal and Rietveld, 1994 for the Netherlands).

Conclusion

We have developed a search model for two-earner households and derived the properties of the decision rules which determine the job or residential moving behaviour. The search model makes several predictions about job and residential behaviour of two-earner households. According to the search model, the commuting distance and the distance between the workplaces of the wage earners of the household both positively affect job mobility, while the wage rate negatively affects job mobility. Moreover, the model implies that in general, two-earner households move job less often than single wage-earners.

Notes

[1] For an analysis of the relationship between residential and job moving decisions for single wage-earners, see, inter alia, Weinberg, 1979; Linneman and Graves, 1983; Zax, 1991, 1994 and Chapter 3.

[2] In the empirical applications of commuting behaviour analysis, moving behaviour is not ignored. For example, White (1986) uses the variable 'elapsed residential duration' - which measures differences in residential mobility - as a regressor. Madden (1981) uses the variable 'elapsed job duration', arguing that 'workers expecting a high rate of job turnover will tend to locate their residences based on the spatial distribution of all potential employers, but workers expecting longer job tenure will tend to locate their residences on the basis of a specific job location'.

[3] Variables which are associated with wage earner 1 and 2 are denoted by the subscript 1 and 2 respectively.

[4] For example, one might distinguish between v_1, the utility experienced by wage earner 1, and v_2, the utility experienced by wage earner 2. Suppose that $v_1 = w_1 - z_1 + r$ and $v_2 = w_2 - z_2 + r$. Then v might be equal to $v_1 + v_2$ - i.e. v_1 and v_2 are perfect substitutes - or equal to $(v_1 * v_2)^{0.5}$.

[5] The results in this chapter are not affected by this assumption.

[6] Some households will search for residences closer to employment centres as they realise that the probability of obtaining job offers with small commuting distances is increased. Unfortunately, search models then become spatially non-stationary and therefore analytically intractable (see Maier, 1995). Given these limitations, we assume that the probability of receiving an offer and the distribution f do not depend on the current spatial residence or workplace location.

[7] For example, the wage distribution may depend on the educational level.

[8] For i,j,k = 1,2,3, the following condition should hold: $|z_i - z_j| < z_k < z_i + z_j$ ($i \neq j \neq k$).

[9] In the present chapter, we focus on members of two-earner households who make changes in the labour market by moving from one job to another; other labour market transitions are excluded. One may extend the model presented here allowing for involuntary job moves. It can be shown that the theoretical results are not qualitatively affected. For a formal treatment of this extension in a more elementary search model with one single wage-earner, see Chapter 3.

[10] Moreover, for the case of earning couples, this decision does not depend on z_3 while lifetime utility $V(w_1,z_1,w_2,z_2,r,z_3)$ does depend on z_3.

[11] The hazard rate at t is defined as the rate at which a transition occurs at t, conditional on survival up to t.

[12] The theoretical effects of the characteristics reported here can be used to interpret empirical investigations. For example, the effects of wages, commuting distance and the distance between

the workplaces on the hazard rates of moving job can be empirically examined (see the empirical part of this study).

[13] If the probability that the nonemployed worker would enter the labour market is much smaller than the probability that the employed worker changes job (so θ_{w2}/θ_{w1} is small) or is much smaller than the probability that the household changes residence (so θ_{w2}/θ_r is small), then the type 1 household can be treated as a type 2 household. The same seems true if the expected labour contribution of one wage earner to lifetime utility is small.

[14] For example, on average, women have older spouses, who entered the labour market earlier; women earn less, so the contribution to the total household income is less; it is more common for women with young children to leave the labour market and re-enter the labour market after a couple of years; women work more part-time and, finally, women are more likely to have a spouse who is in the labour market.

[15] This seems to be a safe assumption for the average person in the Netherlands. The mean commuting distance is about 20 kilometres and jobs are offered within a range of 100 kilometres.

Appendix 4.1 The Effect of z_3 on the Distribution of z_1 and z_2

The effect of a change in z_3 on the distribution of z_1 and z_2 can easily be shown in a diagram. We make clear that

$$\frac{\partial F_{z_1,z_2}(z_1,z_2 \mid z_3)}{\partial z_3} < 0$$

Below, we have drawn z_1, z_2 and z_3. The surface area of the overlapping circles is equal to $F_{z_1,z_2}(z_1,z_2 \mid z_3)$. By increasing z_3, the area shrinks, so $F_{z_1,z_2}(z_1,z_2 \mid z_3)$ decreases.

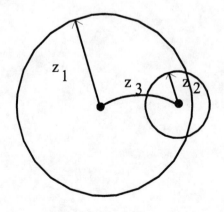

Figure 4.2

5. Commuting: In Search of Jobs and Residences

Introduction

Most studies which focus on commuting behaviour take for granted that uncertainty about finding new dwellings or jobs does not play a role, implying that individuals need not search for dwellings and houses because they are fully informed. This is in clear contrast to the model presented in chapter 3. In the present chapter therefore we use a simplified version of the model presented in chapter 3 and we examine the influence of relocation behaviour on commuting behaviour in a model with market imperfections.[1] For example, we will demonstrate that due to market imperfections, workers may be discouraged to decrease the current commuting distance by means of a job or residential move. The structure of this chapter is as follows. We first introduce a simplified version of the model presented in chapter 3. Next, we investigate some special properties of the model. Then we discuss the effect of the geographical structure on commuting behaviour.

The Search Model

The basic assumption of the search model is that a job is entirely characterised by the wage w and the commuting costs z. Similarly, a dwelling is characterised by the place utility r and the commuting costs.[2] The point of departure in this chapter is that the workers search continuously for better jobs and dwellings, maximising the discounted future flow of wages and place utilities minus commuting costs, taking into account the once-only costs of moving jobs c_1, and residences c_2. Workers receive job and residential offers with a fixed probability in every period. The probability of receiving a job offer, p_1, and a dwelling offer, p_2, are supposed to be independent. Job and dwelling offers do not arrive at the same period in time and pooling is not allowed: job and dwelling offers have to be refused or accepted before other offers arrive.

We denote density functions by f_i, ($i=w,r,z$) suppressing in the notation that these functions are conditional on exogenous characteristics. Individuals face a geographical distribution of employers and dwellings, which is not necessarily uniform. Wage and commuting costs offers are random drawings from a wage offer density function $f_w(w)$ and a commuting costs density function $f_z(z)$. $f_w(w)$ and $f_z(z)$ may be dependent. Similarly, place utility and commuting costs offers are random drawings from a place utility offer density function $f_r(r)$ and a commuting costs density function $f_z(z)$, which are also allowed to be dependent. The wage w, is received until a new job is accepted; similarly, the place utility r is experienced until the individual changes residence. The commuting costs z, are borne until either a new job or residence is accepted.

We denote the lifetime utility received from the current wage, place utility and commuting costs as $V(w,r,z)$. V includes the possibility of better offers in the future. All benefits - w, r - and costs - z, c_1, c_2 - are discounted at rate ρ. The basic decision that the individual has to take is whether to accept a job or a residential offer, taking into account the expected offers in the future. To distinguish between the current characteristics and the characteristics offered, we add a subscript 'x' to the characteristics offered.

In situation where individuals a receive job and dwelling offers and when both offers may imply a change in the commuting costs, a decision rule has to be constructed such that future offers of *both* types are appropriately taken into account. We can write the decision rules for an individual as follows:

Decision rules

Given a job offer of wage w_x and commuting costs z_x, and given the current wage w, place utility r, commuting costs z, and reservation wage $res_w(w,r,z|z_x)$:

change job   if $w_x > res_w(w,r,z|z_x)$
otherwise do not change job.

Given a residential offer of place utility r_x and commuting costs z_x, and given the current wage w, place utility r, commuting costs z, and reservation place utility $res_r(w,r,z|z_x)$:

change residence   if $r_x > res_r(w,r,z|z_x)$
otherwise do not change residence.

The decision rules define the dynamic maximisation problem, as the individual maximises the lifetime utility V(w,r,z) by choosing optimal values for $res_w(w,r,z|z_x)$ and $res_r(w,r,z|z_x)$. In the sequel, we will suppress that $res_w(w,r,z|z_x)$ and $res_r(w,r,z|z_x)$ depend on the current w,r,z, so we will use $res_w(z_x)$ and $res_r(z_x)$. Note that the decision rules imply that, given a job offer, the worker is interested in (w_x,z_x), viz. the combination of the wage and commuting costs offer, and not in $w_x - z_x$, viz. the wage minus commuting costs. So the job searcher takes into account that the commuting costs can be changed via a residence move, and wage and commuting costs are traded off in an optimal way.

Given the assumptions stated above, the lifetime utility V(w,r,z) can be defined and written as follows:

$$V(w,r,z) =$$

$$\frac{w+r-z+\rho p_1 \int_0^\infty \int_{res_w(y)}^\infty [V(x,r,y)-c_1]f_w(x)dx f_z(y)dy + \rho p_2 \int_0^\infty \int_{res_r(y)}^\infty [V(w,x,y)-c_2]f_r(x)dx f_z(y)dy}{1-\rho+\rho p_1[1-\int_0^\infty F_w(res_w(y))f_z(y)dy] + \rho p_2[1-\int_0^\infty F_r(res_r(y))f_z(y)dy]}$$

This expression for V(w,r,z) can be explained as follows. The numerator of V(w,r,z) equals the utility of the present period (w + r - z) plus the discounted future gains of moving job or moving residence in the next period. Costs due to moving job or residence are appropriately subtracted. A job move occurs, conditional on an offer which arrives with probability p_1, if $w_x > res_w(w,r,z|z_x)$. A residential move occurs, conditional on an offer which arrives with probability p_2, if $r_x > res_r(w,r,z|z_x)$. The denominator of V(w,r,z) discounts the sum of current utility and expected gain according to the length of stay in the current position as it can be written as 1 − ρ(1 − Probability to move residence − Probability to move job).

Properties of the Search Model

Compensation for Commuting

It is a standard assumption in the economic literature that commuting costs are compensated either by lower housing prices (viz. higher place utility) or by higher wages (see Zax, 1991b). We will make clear however that according to the dynamic model proposed, it is straightforward to see that the current commuting costs may be compensated by *future* wages or *future* place utilities which are obtained via future job or residence relocations.

Let us consider a equal marginal increase in the wage and in the commuting costs. Clearly, this does not affect the current instantaneous utility, however this will affect lifetime utility via moving behaviour.[3] We denote the change in lifetime utility due to a marginal increase in the wage and in the commuting costs as V_{w+z}, so $V_{w+z} = \partial V/\partial w + \partial V/\partial z$. Given the dynamic model specified - and using the first-order conditions with respect to res_r and res_w, V_{w+z} can be written as:

$$V_{w+z} = \frac{\rho p_2 \int_0^\infty \int_{res_r(y)}^\infty \frac{\partial V(w,x,y)}{\partial w} f_r(x)dx f_z(y)dy}{1-\rho+\rho p_1[1-\int_0^\infty F_w(res_w(y))f_z(y)dy]+[\rho p_2 1-\int_0^\infty F_r(res_r(y))f_z(y)dy]}$$

The numerator of this expression may be interpreted as the discounted weighted increase in life time utility due to the increase in wage after a residential move. It is important to note that V_{w+z} is non-negative (because $\partial V/\partial w > 0$). If and only if the probability of moving residence in the future is zero (so $p_2 = 0$, or $res_r(y) \to \infty$ for all y), then V_{w+z} equals zero, otherwise $V_{w+z} > 0$. The denominator of this expression has the same interpretation as the denominator of $V(w,r,z)$.

The increase in lifetime utility due to a equal marginal increase in the wage and in the commuting costs arises, because commuting costs vary due to residence and job moves, while wages vary only due to job moves. In other words, the value of the current commuting costs does not affect lifetime utility after a future residential move, but the current wage still does. Consequently, workers who are mobile in the housing market benefit more from a marginal increase in the wage and in the commuting costs than those who are not. As a result, the common result that commuters are compensated in the labour or housing market does not hold if market imperfections are prevalent. *Due to market imperfections, individuals will accept commuting costs which are compensated by future wages or future place utilities which may be obtained by future job or residence relocations.*

Similarly, it can be shown that the change in lifetime utility given a marginal increase in the place utility and in the commuting costs, V_{r+z}, is non-negative; only if the probability to move job is zero, then V_{r+z} is zero.

Comparative Statics

We have made clear above that workers who may move in the housing market gain more from a simultaneous increase in commuting costs and wages than those who are not mobile. This raises the question how this gain depends on the structural parameters in the model. For example, one may hypothesise that those workers with higher residential moving costs c_2 gain to a lesser extent than other workers from a simultaneous increase in wage and commuting costs. Similarly, it is plausible that those with lower probabilities of receiving a residential offer p_2 (e.g. due to discrimination) gain less. Unfortunately, we are not able to show this formally. To get more insight, we rely on simulations to do comparative statics which enables us to check whether these hypotheses hold in general. We found that although the simulations confirmed that the effects are ambiguous, it appears indeed that it is in general the case that $\partial V_{w+z}/\partial p_2 > 0$ and $\partial V_{w+z}/\partial c_2 < 0$ (for details on the simulations, see Appendix 5.1).[4] In case that $p_2 = 0$, V_{w+z} is, of course, zero, while V_{w+z} obtains its maximum if $p_2 = 1$. So the intuitive result that individuals who receive more residential offers will gain more from a simultaneous increase in wages and commuting costs holds in general. In Figure 5.1, we show the results of the simulations with respect to p_2 (simulations with respect to c_2 show that in general V_{w+z} decreases as c_2 increases).

As can for example also be seen in 0, it seems in general to be the case that $\partial^2 V_{w+z}/\partial p_2^2 < 0$. This implies that a marginal increase in p_2 has a strong effect on V_{w+z} in case p_2 is low. This has some interesting implications. For example, the Dutch housing market has traditionally been highly regulated by government regulations. This has led, among other things, to low residential flowing rates and therefore to a very low probability of receiving a residential offer (in particular for those who are eligible for a subsidised dwelling). According to the results, changes in the regulations such that the residential flow rate will increase, will likely lead to a (substantial) increase in welfare as the negative effects of commuting will be more readily reduced by moving residence.

It is also interesting to compare V_{w+z} with V_w ($= \partial V / \partial w$) for different values of p_2 (see Figure 5.1). The difference between V_{w+z} and V_w equals the loss in lifetime utility due to a marginal increase in z. As expected, this loss is minimal for $p_2 = 1$, as for this case the worker is maximally able to reduce the commuting costs.[5]

Acceptance Behaviour

The obtained result that mobile commuters do not demand full compensation for current commuting suggests intuitively that those workers who are more mobile in the housing market demand *less* compensation (in form of wages) for commuting than others, and are therefore more likely to accept a job offer.

We will explain here that this intuition is misleading: workers who are more mobile in the housing market may demand higher wages than those who are not.[6] To clarify this 'paradoxical' result, we approximate the 'reservation wage' of an individual in the labour market by using a Taylor expansion, so $res_w(w,r,z|z_x) = res_w(w,r,z) + z_x.a(w,z,r)$. So the decision rule reads:

change job   if $w_x - z_x.a(w,z,r) > res_w(w,r,z)$;
otherwise do not change job

The parameter $a(w,z,r)$ weighs the change in the commuting costs, where $0 < a(w,z,r) \leq 1$. Only if the worker has no opportunity to change commuting costs by moving residence (e.g. $p_2 = 0$), then $a(w,z,r) = 1$.[7] If in this case the job moving costs c_1 are equal to zero, then res_w equals $w - z$, and the decision rule reads: accept a job if $w_x - z_x > w - z$, otherwise do not accept. We will denote the reservation wage of a worker with fixed residential location as res_{wf}, so $res_{wf} = w - z + z_x$.

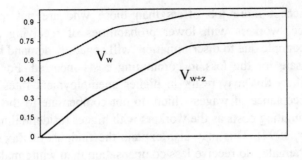

$$p_2$$

**Figure 5.1 Marginal changes in lifetime utility
V as functions of p_2,
the probability tó receive a residential offer**

In Figure 5.1, we have drawn an example of a job acceptance region of a worker with fixed residential location (the shaded area above the reservation wage res_{wf}). We have also drawn an example of a job acceptance region of a worker who may move residence with a certain positive probability (the region above the reservation wage res_w). One may show that for $z_x = 0$, res_w > res_{wf}. Hence, as $a(w,z,r) < 1$ for the worker who may move residence, res_{wf} and res_w intersect at $z_x > 0$. The implication of this result is clear: if a job is offered for which holds that the commuting costs are low, then this will induce the mobile worker to demand *more* wage than the worker would do with a fixed residential location.

The explanation for this result is that in case of a positive probability to move residence, z_x will more likely increase after a residential move. To reduce this risk, the worker will increase the reservation wage and wait for a better offer. The implications of this result may be serious: the combination of uncertainty (about future moving behaviour) and the existence of moving costs may discourage workers to decrease commuting costs. On the other hand, if the commuting costs offered are high, then this will induce the mobile worker to demand *less* wage than the worker with a fixed residential location. Hence, whether workers who are more mobile in the housing market demand higher wages than those who are not depends on the value of the commuting costs offered.

Note, however, that for most workers the probability of receiving a large commuting cost offer is much larger than receiving a low commuting cost offer.[8] So workers who have small residential moving costs and/or high residential arrival pro will demand less compensation for most jobs offered and will accept more job offers than those who are not mobile. As a consequence, workers with lower probabilities of receiving a residential offer, for example due to discrimination, will generally demand higher wages to compensate for the loss in commuting costs incurred. For competitive labour markets this may result in higher unemployment rates and a more frequent acceptance of wages which do not compensate to the same extent for the commuting costs as the workers with higher residential mobility rates (see Holzer, 1994). This may also explain the findings of Zax (1991a) that blacks and females do receive less compensation than white males, as blacks and females are more restricted in the housing market. This result also concurs with the notion that given a relocation of an employer, it is much more likely that those with low residential moving rates will leave the current employer (see Zax, 1991b; Zax and Kain, 1991).

In line with the model individuals will differ in their commuting behaviour due to differences in moving costs and in the probability to receive an offer. Clearly, individuals who have lower moving costs and who are more likely to receive an offer reach better positions at lower (moving or waiting) costs, and are therefore more able to reach a more favourable situation *as time passes*. So the search model specified is consistent with the common view that persons with a greater ability to adapt their housing situation to their work locations will have shorter commuting distances (see Rouwendal and Rietveld (1994), or higher wages (see Van den Berg, 1992) and is also consistent with the view that persons with a greater ability to adapt their housing situation to their work locations (e.g. young persons) will *temporarily* accept larger commuting distances as they will be compensated in the future. In the empirical investigation, we will come back to this issue.

Until now, we did not discuss the effect of exogenous differences in the disutility of commuting. However, there are many reasons to expect that individuals differ in this respect (see, for example, Van den Berg and Gorter, 1997). For example, married women may have a higher disutility of commuting due to higher household responsibilities (see Madden, 1981). Even small differences in the disutility of commuting are thought to have large consequences for the behaviour in the labour or housing market, as it reduces the opportunity to receive an acceptable offer substantially.[9] However, in case a person is mobile in both the labour and housing market this effect will be weaker. As a consequence, differences in the disutility of commuting will particularly have an effect on the acceptance behaviour in one market as the moving in the other market is restricted.

The relationship between residential moving, job moving and commuting behaviour depends on the geographical structure of the economy (see Zax (1994). The geographical structure is captured in the model via $f_z(z)$, the distribution of commuting distances. To improve an understanding of the effect of the geographical structure on commuting, we will distinguish 3 stereotypes:

(*i*)   an urban area with one CBD (Central Business District); the dwellings are distributed around the CBD. This stereotype traditionally used to characterise the geographical structure of large American cities.

(*ii*)   A region where employment and residential locations are homogeneously distributed over space.

(*iii*)   A region which consists of overlapping urban areas. Overlapping urban areas can be typified by many employment centres which are near to each other and where each employment centre is surrounded by residential areas. This type of geographical structure is more common in the Netherlands and Germany.

The essential characteristic of an urban area with one CBD is that all workplace locations are concentrated in one location; hence the commuting costs are fully determined by the residential location (so $z_x = z$ given a job offer). As a consequence, the reservation wage rule can be written as: accept a job offer, if $w_x - z > res_w(w - z)$. This implies that the worker is merely interested in the difference between the wage and the commuting costs.[10] The reservation wage res_w does not then depend on the current place utility and commuting costs, and the reservation place utility res_r does not depend on the wage.[11] In this type of geographical structure, individuals will ask full compensation for commuting based on *current* characteristics.[12]

Whenever workers face a homogenous distribution of employers and dwellings (stereotype (ii), *every* future job or residential offer implies a change in the commuting costs. In the case where employers and dwellings are geographically concentrated (type (iii), future relocations of job and residence will be less influential compared to the situation when workers face a homogenous distribution of employers and dwellings, because it will be more likely that either the new residence or the new job is located near the current residence or job respectively.

Consequently, one of the implications of the search model is that if potential employers and dwellings are more homogeneously distributed over space, future job and residence relocations are more important as a factor which determines commuting behaviour. In the case when merely the workplace location is fixed, job mobility does not affect commuting behaviour. This elementary result might have consequences for commuting behaviour (and modelling of commuting behaviour) in the near future: current trends in many developed countries show that employers suburbanise such that potential workplace locations become more scattered over space. Similar trends are observable for the residential location of households. These trends indicate that the distribution may become more homogeneous. This implies that the possibility of future job and residence relocations will become more significant as decisive factors which determine present day commuting behaviour.

Conclusion

In this chapter we have examined the influence of relocation behaviour on commuting behaviour in a model with market imperfections (imperfect information, moving costs). We relied on search theory to describe the behaviour of workers in the labour and housing market. The major result of this chapter is that it demonstrates that workers voluntarily accept commuting costs which are not compensated for by the current characteristics of jobs and residences. The reason for this is that workers realise that commuting costs are temporary because they may move job or residence in the future.

The result that commuters do not demand full compensation for current commuting suggests that those workers who are more mobile in the housing market demand *less* compensation (in the form of wages) for commuting than others, and are therefore more likely to accept a job offer. This intuition is misleading: workers who are more mobile in the housing market may demand higher wages than those who are not as they reject job offer nearby. This result may be closely related to the conclusion of Hamilton (1982, 1989) that, due to market imperfections, workers are nowadays 'footloose'.

We also discussed the effect of the geographical structure on commuting behaviour according to the search model. One of the implications of the search model is that if potential employers and dwellings are more homogeneously distributed over space, future job and residence relocations are more significant as a factor which determine commuting behaviour.

Notes

[1] In short: this model is a special case of the model introduced in Chapter 3, as it excludes the probability of becoming nonemployed and we make stronger assumption on the functional form of the instantaneous utility function. Another difference is that we treat the decision process in discrete time and interpret the variable 'z' as commuting costs instead of commuting distance. These differences do not concern us.

[2] Place utility is defined as the monetarised utility of the dwelling experienced by an individual minus the commuting costs. Hence place utility is negatively related to the housing price.

[3] The instantaneous utility equals $w + r - z$. So $\partial(w + r - z)/\partial w + \partial(w + r - z)/\partial z = 0$.

[4] For example, we found a few instances where $\partial V_{w+z}/\partial p_2$ is slightly negative, but for all simulations, we found that V_{w+z} obtains its minimum when $p_2 = 0$ and its maximum when $p_2 = 1$.

[5] This loss is not zero, because the waiting and residential moving costs are positive.

[6] We distinguish between the extreme case that residential mobility is zero ($p_2 = 0$) and residential mobility is positive ($p_2 > 0$).

[7] If the searcher is confident that next period he/she will receive an acceptable residence offer at zero distance from the new job, then a(w, z, r) approaches zero.

[8] For example, suppose that employment is uniformly distributed over space. Let us consider a median worker of whom the *current* commuting distance is 1/5 of the maximum of the commuting distances offered. The probability that a job offer will reduce the current commuting distance is then for this case equal to 0.04. Hence, the probability of receiving an attractive job offer (in terms of wages) at a large commuting distance is usually much higher than receiving an attractive offer nearby.

[9] The probability of accepting a job offer depends on the set of acceptable workplace locations which is two-dimensional, while commuting distance is one-dimensional, so the probability of accepting an offer increases approximately quadratic in accepted commuting distance given the residence location (see Rouwendal and Rietveld, 1994; Seater, 1979).

[10] In case $c_1 = 0$ then $res_w(w-z) = w-z$.

[11] Note that in this model, the demand for housing does not depend on the wage.

[12] In all other - nowadays more realistic - cases that employers are also located outside the CBD, individuals' commuting behaviour will be affected by the location of the employer.

Appendix 5.1 Simulations

We have run simulations with the search model using the following method. The lifetime utility V(w, r, z) can be calculated by approximating the distributions F_i at N_i (i=w, r, d) finite points w, r and z for any arbitrary acceptance rule. Simulations with the search model proceed then as follows. First, given the exogenous values of the structural parameters and an arbitrary acceptance rule (e.g. reject all offers), the lifetime utility V for all values of w, r and z is calculated. In the search model specified, lifetime utility V of accepted states depends on all future moves. So the lifetime utility V(w, r, z) has to be calculated simultaneously for all values of w, r, z, because the value of V(w,r,z) depends on all V(w', r', z') for arbitrary w', r' and z'. Given N ($=N_w.N_r.N_z$) different combinations of w, r, z and given the acceptance rule, lifetime utility V can be obtained by means of an iterative procedure which solves a system of N non-linear equations. Second, the optimal acceptance rule which maximises V can be obtained by comparing the values V of different acceptance rules. The optimal acceptance rule is the rule which maximises V.

For all simulations reported, we have made the assumption that F_w, F_r and F_z are all discrete uniform distributions. Computing time of the simulations increases exponentially in N. In order to keep the simulation time limited for the basic model, we compared the outcome of a few models with different number of combinations. It appeared that even for $N_w=2$, $N_r=2$ and $N_z=2$, interesting results could be obtained, but that computing time is still short for $N_w=3$, $N_r=2$ and $N_z=6$. Therefore, we assumed for the basic model that there exists two different values for place utility (r =50,100), six different values for the commuting costs (z= 25,50,75,...,150) and 3 different values for the wage (w = 100,200,300). Furthermore, we assumed that the cost of moving job equals 100 and the costs of moving residence is 100. The probability of receiving a job offer and the probability of receiving a residence offer are set equal to 0.2. The acceptance behaviour of an individual is investigated who has a current wage of 100, a current place utility of 50, and current commuting costs of 50.

The comparative static results were obtained as follows: we calculated the job and residential mobility acceptance probability for an individual for a range of different values for the probability of receiving a residence offer and for a range of different values of moving residential moving costs.

PART III

EMPIRICAL APPLICATION OF MOVING BEHAVIOUR AND COMMUTING

6. Are Job-to-Job Mobility, Residential Mobility and Commuting Related?

Introduction

The debate among economists on the relationship between residence and workplace relocation is for many years still vivid. Firstly, economic theory is still in a stage of further analytical development, instigated inter alia by new insights acquired in the fields of migration and labour market research (Linneman and Graves, 1983; Zax, 1991). Secondly, many empirical issues are still unresolved and do lead to inconclusive interpretations. This is likely due to differences in the geographical pattern and the socio-demographic structure of the various (regional or urban) economies. Accordingly, various economic theories are needed to explain the relationship between residence, workplace relocation and commuting which depend explicitly on the geographical structure of the economy. In particular, the distinction between non-overlapping urban areas, dominant in the United States, and overlapping urban areas, like the Netherlands or the Ruhr area in Germany, is of critical importance here.

It has been strongly argued by geographers and economists alike that the type of relationship between voluntary job-to-job mobility and residential mobility depends on the size of the distance of the moves considered by the individual or the household (Roseman, 1971; Zax, 1994). Clearly, a residential move within the same city has different consequences than a move to another city hundred kilometres away. Recently, for non-overlapping urban areas, an interesting micro-economic foundation has been offered for this argument (Zax, 1994). It can, for instance, be shown that - given the structure of an urban economy - job and residential moves may act as substitutes given an unexpected change in the commuting costs, in particular when the employer moves the workplace location (Zax,

1991,1994). This result has been supported by empirical evidence (Zax, 1991; Zax and Kain, 1991). In contrast, it has been taken for granted that for workers who migrate between (non-overlapping) urban areas over long distances, there is hardly any meaningful distinction between a job or residential move, as both are envisaged as necessary complements. Consequently, for non-overlapping urban areas, it seems necessary to distinguish between intra- and inter-regional moves.

For relatively more homogeneous overlapping urban areas (and rural areas), however, a different economic framework is needed which can deal with a different type of combinations of workplace and residence locations, including those in (seemingly) distinct urban areas. Moreover, in overlapping urban areas which include a set of open labour markets, the distinction between intra- and inter-regional mobility seems ad-hoc and, therefore, less meaningful. First of all, borders between urban areas are difficult to draw as urban areas are not surrounded by rural areas. Secondly, whether a move is 'intra-regional' or 'inter-regional' depends on the characteristics of the individual, and therefore has to be *explained* by economic theory. In the present paper, we will rely on a search theoretic framework which illuminates the link between moves at different geographical scales.

For example, let us focus on the Netherlands. The Dutch labour market consists of distinct though partially overlapping regional labour markets. This structure restricts the use of urban models to understand commuting behaviour. A core assumption of urban models is that wage and rent gradients determine the choice of the residence location, and the distance is therefore optimally chosen (White, 1988; Wheaton, 1974; Zax, 1991, 1994). However, in the Netherlands, wage gradients have never been empirically identified and are, most likely, minimal or even absent. This is probably due to many wage-setting regulations set by the government, the absence of central business districts, and the geographical structure of the Netherlands which consists of many relatively small cities. For example, the commuting time between the centres of the two largest cities in the Netherlands, Amsterdam and Rotterdam, is about one hour. The area between these two cities is however not rural and offers many job opportunities. For example, commuters between these cities travel via Den Haag. Furthermore, in the Netherlands, rent gradients are flatter than in other countries. This can be explained by the outer geographical structure and the involvement of the Dutch government in the housing market. First, the majority of new house owners and tenants receive subsidies. Second, the renting markets, which cover the majority of the dwellings in the Netherlands, is subject to a form of price regulation (Van der Schaar, 1991). Often, the rent paid is completely determined by the government. Moreover, many properties are owned by housing associations that use waiting lists and do not supply the property to the highest bidder. In conclusion, the use of urban models, which heavily rely on wage and rent gradients would have severe limitations in this context.

In the present chapter, we will analyse the relationship between residence and job-to-job mobility. To simplify matters, we use a theory that does not rely on the existence of wage or rent gradients (Rouwendal, 1994). We will choose our starting point in recent developments in the literature which emphasise the importance of residential moving costs (see, inter alia, Zax, 1991, 1994; Boehm, 1981; Ioannides, 1987) and job moving costs (see, inter alia, Hughes and McCormick, 1985; Van den Berg, 1992). Therefore, we will pursue the theoretical analysis by assuming that individuals consider job or residence relocations, while taking into account that residence and job relocations are costly. Furthermore, in contrast to the existing literature on the relationship between job and residential mobility, we acknowledge that individuals may move more than once in the future, and that jobs and residences are accepted, given an appropriate job or residence offer. So, the type of dynamic decision-making we consider here is explicitly dynamic, and fits directly in the nowadays popular search theory. According to this model, workers do not choose the optimal commuting distance by maximising current utility, due to moving costs and uncertainty about future relocations. In contrast, workers consider whether a job or residential move, which may change the commuting distance, will increase lifetime utility. The search model considered in this paper implies therefore types of mobility depend positively on commuting costs. In the present paper we will examine job and residential mobility simultaneously.

The statistical analysis of simultaneous (spatial) choices is however not always straightforward. Zax (1994) gives a short overview of different econometric techniques which can handle the simultaneity of workplace and residence relocations. Empirical studies on the interrelationship between residence and workplace relocation based on micro data can be found, inter alia, in Bartel (1979), Linneman and Graves (1983) and Zax (1991). These studies rely on static discrete choice models, who employed duration techniques, because of the restricted type of data at hand. Zax's (1994) overview paper suggests that bivariate discrete choice models are appropriate if the distinction between intra- and inter-regional mobility is ignored. However, in general, the natural method to estimate search models is in continuous time. In this paper, we will investigate whether residential and voluntary job-to-job mobility are related by employing a bivariate duration model. We compare the results of the bivariate duration model with a bivariate discrete choice model, because application of different techniques may give us more confidence in the sensitivity of the results with respect to the chosen specification.

The paper is organised as follows. First we discuss the relationship between job and residential mobility. Then we will present the specifications of the loglikelihood of the duration model and the discrete choice model. Next, the empirical results of the bivariate discrete choice and duration models are presented and compared, based on a sample from the Netherlands. Finally, we offer a concluding section.

The Dependence Between Job and Residential Mobility

To get a better understanding of the relationship between commuting, job-to-job mobility and residential mobility in a general setting, we will use here a stationary search model. In contrast to the static utility theories, which traditionally have dominated the discussion on the relationship between job and residences, it is assumed that one has to search for jobs and residences. In line with the search literature, it is supposed that jobs and dwellings are offered with a probability which depends on the search effort in the labour and housing markets. The individual has to decide instantly whether or not to accept a job or residence offer, taking into account (the change in) commuting costs. The use of search theory seems obvious, since it has been one of the main theoretical and empirical tools to understand transitions in the labour market (see Devine and Kiefer, 1993). In some cases, search theory can explain empirical facts in commuting behaviour which are hard to explain using static utility theory. For example, Hamilton's (1982) results suggest that a random matching model of jobs and workers in urban areas is closer to the reality of urban commuting than the urban economic model with decentralised employment. Rouwendal (1994) shows that theories which include search by unemployed and employers are able to underpin Hamilton's (1982) finding that workers are virtually footloose. Although search theory has been less influential in explaining residential mobility behaviour, researchers have become increasingly interested in this new research endeavour (Pickles and Davies, 1991; Rouwendal, 1991).

According to the search model developed, behaviour on the labour and residence market are related, as every job or residential move might imply a change in the commuting costs. Furthermore, it is assumed that jobs can be characterised by the wage rate (Define and Kiefer, 1993), and residences by 'place utility' (Wolpert, 1965; Yapa, Polese and Wolpert, 1971). The distributions of wages, place utility and commuting costs are supposed to be known to the worker. So, in essence, workers change job, because they have found a match which offers a higher wage, while they change residence, because they have found a better match - a higher place utility - between their demand for dwellings, which is individual specific, and the supply of dwellings. Of course, each combination of dwelling and job location uniquely determines the commuting costs. As it is explicitly assumed that individuals take into account future residential and job moves, our analysis is truly dynamic.

Whether an individual accepts a residence or job offer does not only depend on the direct gain in wage or place utility, but also on the residence and job moving cost. As far as we know, no clear empirical estimates of the level of generalised costs of moving residence are available, but the residential moving costs are likely high (Boehm, 1981; Weinberg Friedman and Mayo, 1981; Amundsen, 1985; Ioannides, 1987; Pickles and Davies,1991; Bartik, Butler and Liu, 1992). It is noteworthy that in contrast, the results of Van den Berg (1992) suggest that job turnover costs are low. In the search model considered, we allow explicitly for the costs associated with moving job and residence.

The point of departure in our analysis is that the workers search continuously for better jobs and dwellings, maximising the discounted future flow of wages, place utilities, minus commuting costs, taking into account the costs of changing jobs and residences. So, job and residential moving behaviour and commuting behaviour are due to a combination of chance - the arrival of an offer - and a decision-making process - the decision to search with a certain intensity and to accept or reject an offer. So, search theory implies that, in general, a worker is not able to choose the amount of commuting costs which is optimal, due to the existence of relocation costs and the small probability to get a job or residence offered at any desired commuting distance. Search theory is therefore for our purpose an appealing framework as it is based on the idea that individuals accept simultaneously a new combination of a job, residence and commuting distance taking into account future behaviour. Of course, the decision to accept a new job does not only depend on the characteristics of the individual in the labour market, but also on the characteristics of the housing market, while the decisions in the housing market depend also on the characteristics of the individual in the labour market. Consequently, acceptance of a job depends therefore on the level of the residential moving costs and the probability to get a residence offered.

Since no distinction has been made between 'intra-regional' and 'inter-regional' moves, the search theoretic framework presented here can handle different types of job and residence (re)locations. In particular, non-trivial results can be derived about the relationship between 'intra-regional' and 'inter-regional' moves. We will illustrate this by two interesting examples.

Example 1 According to the search model, a move to another residence in the same neighbourhood will occur only if a higher place utility is attained. After the occurrence of the 'intra-regional' move, the probability of an 'inter-regional' residential move will decrease, because the willingness to move residence again has declined. Consequently, individuals with higher probabilities of accepting 'inter-regional' job offers will, in general, move less 'intra-regionally'.

Example 2 Consider the situation that an individual is offered a job on an 'inter-regional' distance of hundreds of kilometres. According to the search model, if the individual accepts the job offer, then this implies that (almost) every residence offer will be accepted with probability one, reducing the long 'commuting distance' as quickly as possible. However, after the inter-regional residential move, the probability of moving residence again will likely be higher than before, as the place utility of the dwelling offered first will be, on average, low. This well-known phenomenon, called 'repeat migration' (DaVanzo, 1981), can therefore be understood based on simple search theoretic assumptions.

With the following two examples, we will make clear that the introduction of search theory sheds also new light on a range of some other aspects of commuting behaviour, which are hard to explain using static theories. *Example 3* Search theory recognises that it takes time to obtain desirable employment or residence positions by means of moving job or residence. So, ceteris paribus, those who are longer in the labour market are more likely to obtain job positions which offer higher wages and less commuting costs. As a result, the model predicts that older workers are more likely to commute less. This theoretical result corresponds indeed to earlier empirical findings (Rouwendal and Rietveld, 1994).

Example 4 In a study on gender differences and commuting behaviour, White (1986) reports that ('contrary to expectations') commuting distance depends negatively on the elapsed residence duration. However, this result fits neatly within the search framework proposed. The search model predicts that the probability to move residence falls with commuting costs, so individuals with short commuting distances will be observed with large elapsed durations.

According to the search model, job-to-job and residential mobility are related, because they both depend on commuting costs. This implies, of course, that given a reduced form model, job and residential mobility are not related, conditional on commuting costs. Furthermore, a prediction of the search model is that job and residential mobility increase with commuting costs. Of course, this result is a consequence of the underlying assumption that commuting is costly.

In many theoretical and empirical studies where job and residential moving behaviour is analysed, generally a sequential ordering of the decision to move residence or to change jobs is implicitly assumed: individuals search either for jobs given their residence or individuals search for a new residence given the workplace location. The search framework introduced before allows for search on the housing and job market and thus embodies theories that rely on a sequential ordering.

The natural method to estimate search models is the use of duration models, also called hazard, continuous time or failure time models (Lancaster, 1990; Kalbfleisch and Prentice, 1980). So, to examine the above stated implications of the search model, we have to specify the joint behaviour on the labour and housing market in terms of durations. Alternatively, one can treat the duration observations as the outcome of T binary outcomes during T periods. So, a period in which not a move is observed corresponds to a zero, while a move corresponds to a one. If the period chosen is small enough, the continuous time and duration model are in principle equivalent; however, computationally acceptable specifications are different in practice. For example, the handling of endogenous and unobserved variables is not equivalent. So, we will apply bivariate probit and duration models. This gives us the opportunity to check whether the results are robust with respect to the chosen specification.

In contrast to static models, dynamic search models make predictions about expected behaviour in continuous time. So, the search model allows one to calculate the expected duration of the current combination of job and residence. Of course, the expected duration depends explicitly on the parameters of the model, viz. the probability that a residence or a job is offered, the distribution of wages, place utilities and commuting costs, the residential and job moving costs, the discount rate and the current value of the wage, place utility and commuting costs. Using the empirical estimates of job and residential mobility, we will calculate the elasticity of the expected duration of the current combination of residence and job with respect to the commuting costs.

The Specification of the Loglikelihood for Duration and Discrete Choice Panel Observations

Introduction

The natural method to estimate search models is the use of duration models, also called hazard, continuous time or failure time models (Lancaster, 1990; Kalbfleisch and Prentice, 1980). So, to examine the above stated implications of the search model, we have to specify the joint behaviour on the labour and housing market in terms of durations. As an alternative, the duration of stay can be seen as the outcome of a sequence of discrete choices over time. So, one can treat the duration observations as the outcome of T binary outcomes during T periods. A period in which not a move is observed corresponds to a zero, while a move corresponds to a one. This allows for the analysis of durations by means of discrete choice models. It seems natural to analyse discrete data by means of a probit or logit model. However, the parameters and functional form of these models are not invariant to the time unit chosen (Flinn and Heckman, 1982). If the period chosen is small enough however, the continuous time and duration model are in principle equivalent; however, computationally acceptable specifications are different in practice. For example, the handling of endogenous and unobserved variables is not equivalent. So, we will apply bivariate probit and duration models. This gives the opportunity to check whether the results are robust with respect to the chosen specification.

Duration Models

In this section, we construct the likelihood for bivariate multiple duration observations sampled from a stock. Hence, we sample a worker at a certain point of time who is employed (and who occupies a residence). So, initially assume that we observe the total length of the job duration t_1 and the residence duration t_2. The relationship between job and residential moving can be estimated. Given the stock sampled deviation observations, one may distinguish between two types of estimation procedures: joint and conditional likelihood procedures. Joint likelihood procedures estimate $F(t_1,t_2)$ given the observed variation in the deviations t_1 and t_2. Conditional likelihood procedures estimate $F(t_1,t_2)$ given the observed variation in the durations t_1 and t_2 conditional on the elapsed duration of p_1 and p_2. We prefer conditional likelihood procedures to joint likelihood procedures, as less strong assumptions are needed about stationarity of the process (Ridder, 1984). The specification of the likelihood of t_1 and t_2, given the elapsed durations p_1 and p_2, will be explained now.

At the moment of sampling, we observe the elapsed job and residence durations (no left censoring). We follow this worker our time until he/she leaves the job.

We denote the bivariate distribution of T_1 and T_2 with completed duration variables t_1 and t_2 as $f(t_1,t_2)$, the corresponding bivariate cumulative distribution as $F(t_1,t_2)$, and the corresponding survival function as $\overline{F}(t_1,t_2)$, defined as the probability of surviving until t_1 and t_2 So

$$\overline{F}(t_1,t_2) = F(t_1) - F(t_2) + F(t_1,t_2)$$

Then, the likelihood of t_1, t_2, conditional on the elapsed durations p_1 and p_2 has then following form:

$$l(t_1 t_2 \mid p_1, p_2) = \frac{f(t_1 t_2)}{\overline{F}(p_1, p_2)}$$

Suppose now that the joint distribution of t_1 and t_2, $f(t_1,t_2)$, depends on the (time-varying) observed variables x and on unobserved variables v_1 and v_2. The durations t_1 and t_2 are independently distributed, given all (observed and unobserved) explanatory variables:

$$f(t_1,t_2|v_1,v_2,x) = f(t_1|v_1,x).f(t_2|v_2,x).$$

So, information about the unobserved variable v_2 cannot improve the statistical description of t_1, given the information about v_1 and x. Similarly, the unobserved variable v_1 cannot improve the statistical description of t_2, given the information about v_2 and x.[1] In other words, the bivariate durations are conditionally independently distributed, the condition being the observed and unobserved explanatory variables. Until now, we have discussed durations. Nevertheless, estimates results are often reported by means of hazard rates (duration models are therefore often called hazard models). The relationship between duration distribution and hazard rate is unique. The hazard rate $\theta(t_i)$ is defined as the probability of leaving the current state at time t_i conditional on being in the current state until t_i $i=1,2$. So $\theta(t_i) = \dfrac{f(t_i)}{1 - F(t_i)}$. We will assume that the hazard rates θ $(t_1|v_1,x)$ and $\theta(t_2|v_2,x)$ corresponding to $f(t_1|v_1,x)$ and $f(t_2|v_2,x)$ respectively, satisfy the following restriction:

$$\theta(t_1|v_1,x) = T(x,\beta_1).v_1$$
$$\theta(t_2|v_2,x) = T(x,\beta_2).v_2$$

where β_1 and β_2 are parameters. We suppose that the mixing function $h(v_1,v_2)$ does not depend on x. We exclude duration-dependency for three different reasons. First, the theoretical search model is stationary. Second, other (univariate) empirical investigations of job and residential mobility in the Netherlands indicate that duration dependency is absent (see Lindeboom and Theeuwes, 1991).[2] Third, studies have reported that there is a trade-off between duration-dependency and the mixing foundation. In essence, when one does not allow for duration-dependency it is more likely unobserved variables affect the hazard rates. Since we will investigate whether the unobserved variables affecting job mobility are related to the unobserved variables affecting residential mobility, it is prudent to assume that duration-dependency is absent. Given this assumption, it appears that:

$$l(t_i) = \theta(t_i).\exp^{-t_i.\theta\,(t_i)} \text{ and } \overline{F}(t_i) = \exp^{-t_i.\theta\,(t_i)} \tag{1}$$

The contribution to the likelihood $l(t_1,t_2|p_1,p_2,x)$ can then be written as:

$$l(t_1,t_2|p_1,p_2,x) = \frac{\displaystyle\int_{v_1 v_2}\!\!\!\int f(t_1|v_1,x).f(t_2|v_2,x).h(v_1,v_2)\,dv_1\,dv_2}{\displaystyle\int_{v_1 v_2}\!\!\!\int \overline{F}(p_1|v_1,x)\overline{F}(p_2|v_2,x)h(v_1,v_2)\,dv_1\,dv_2}$$

Given the choice of a conditional likelihood method, the above equation may be used as a basis for the empirical analysis. In many cases, t_1 is not observed, but it merely known that the some of the durations T_i are larger than a certain value t_i (right-censoring). This may happen because, during the period in which the worker is observed, no transition occurs, or because another transition is made, e.g. an involuntary move. So, different types of observations (censored and complete) have to be included.

Contributions to the likelihood of observations which are right-censored - of which is only known that $T_i > t_i$, $i = 1,2$ - can be easily derived by replacing the densities $f(t_i)$ by survival functions $\overline{F}(t_i)$, $i = 1,2$.

The construction of the loglikelihood for time-stationary explanatory variables is simple, as it just requires substitution of $f(t_1|v_1,x)$ and $f(t_2|v_1,x)$, as defined above in the last equation. However, we wish to include time-varying explanatory variables, since during the period of observation some explanatory variables change. In our specification, we allow the explanatory variables to change annually (episode splitting). This can be established by rewriting the densities of the durations as a multiplication of annually sampled observations.

The likelihood function L of N households which are observed during M years can then be written as follows ($i = 1,..,M$; $j = 1,..,N$):

$$L = \prod_{j=1}^{N} \frac{\displaystyle\int_{v_1 v_2}\!\!\!\int \prod_{i=1}^{M}[f(t_{1ij})^{1-cen_1(ij)}\,\overline{F}(t_{1ij})^{cen_1(ij)}\,f(t_{2ij})^{1-cen_2(ij)}\,\overline{F}(t_{2ij})^{cen_2(ij)}]^{sam_{ij}}\,h(v_1,v_2)\,dv_1\,dv_2}{\displaystyle\int_{v_1 v_2}\!\!\!\int \prod_{i=1}^{M}\overline{F}(p_{1ij})\overline{F}(p_{2ij})]^{sam_{ij}}\,h(v_1,v_2)\,dv_1\,dv_2}$$

where $sam_{ij} = 1$, if individual is sampled in year i, otherwise 0; $cen_1(ij) = 1$, if the job spell of worker j in year i is right-censored, otherwise 0; $cen_2(ij) = 1$, if the residence spell of the worker j in year i is right-censored. Hence, the loglikelihood of t_1,t_2 given time-varying hazard rates can be rewritten simply as the product of stationary conditional densities and survival functions. For further details, we refer to Lancaster (1990).

The choice of the mixing distribution is based on computational and theoretical considerations. Lindeboom and Van den Berg (1994) show in the context of bivariate duration models that results will be substantially liaised when the bivariate mixing function is not flexible enough. Van den Berg, Lindeboom and Ridder (1994) advocate therefore the use of a mixing distribution with discrete masspoints. We follow Van den Berg, Lindeboom and Ridder (1994) and approximate $h(v_1,v_2)$ by a mixing distribution with four discrete masspoints; so both v_1 and v_2 have two points of support (v_1 has v_{11}, v_{12}, and v_2 has v_{21} and v_{22}) with probabilities P_1, P_2, P_3 and P_4 respectively.[3] So

$$P_1 = P(v_1 = v_{11}, v_2 = v_{21}), P_2 = P(v_1 = v_{11}, v_2 = v_{22}),$$
$$P_3 = P(v_1 = v_{12}, v_2 = v_{21}), P_4 = P(v_1 = v_{12}, v_2 = v_{22}).$$

The masspoints and probabilities of the discrete mixing function can then be estimated. Given the estimated masspoints and probabilities of the mixing function, the correlation between the durations can be calculated (Van den Berg, Lindeboom and Ridder, 1994).

The model has been estimated using a maximum likelihood procedure of the program Gauss. Since the loglikelihood does *not* have a unique maximum (Lancaster, 1990), we have estimated the model several times with different starting value for the coefficients.

Discrete Choice Panel Data

The construction of the likelihood of a bivariate probit model in case that data are treated as independent cross-sections is straightforward (Zax, 1991). However, in case of panel data, one should preferably allow for individual specific heterogeneity as it can bias the results (Hsiao, 1986). Similar to the derivation of the likelihood above, allowance for individual-specific unobserved heterogeneity can be established via the use of a mixing function. In the case of discrete choice observations, one may approximate the normal distribution by using Gaussian quadrature approximations (Butler and Moffit, 1982). So, we will estimate the variances of the individual-specific heterogeneity in the job and residential mobility specification by approximating the normal mixing function. So, the loglikelihood can be written as:

$$\prod_{j=1}^{N} \int_{v_1} \int_{v_2} \prod_{i=1}^{M} [P_{ij\,(w,\,r)}^{\,dum_{1ij}}\ P_{ij\,(w,1\,-\,r)}^{\,dum_{2ij}}\ P_{ij\,(1\,-\,w,1\,-\,r)}^{\,dum_{3ij}}\ P_{ij\,(1\,-\,w,\,r)}^{\,dum_{4ij}}\,]^{sam_{ij}}\ h(v_1)h(v_2)dv_1dv$$

where P_{ij} is the probability that the events w and r occur. It is assumed that the occurrences of these events are determined by a bivariate normal distribution. Estimates of the bivariate normal distribution include the correlation between the occurrences of w and r. Let w = 1 denote a job move, otherwise w = 0; and let r = 1 denote a residence move, otherwise r = 0. So, $P_{ij}(w,r)$ is the probability that worker j moves job and residence in year i. h is a standard normal mixing distribution. sam_{ij} = 1, if individual is sampled in year i, otherwise 0; $dum_1(ij)$ = 1, if worker j moves job and residence in year i, otherwise 0; $dum_2(ij)$ = 1, if worker j moves job and does not move residence in year i, otherwise 0; $dum_3(ij)$ = 1, if worker j does not move job and residence in year i, otherwise 0 and $dum_4(ij)$ = 1, if worker j does not move job and moves residence in year i, otherwise 0.

Empirical Application

The data set used here (called Telepanel), collected in 1992-1993, includes the complete life cycle pattern of Dutch respondents, including the labour, residential and family career. The data were collected in a retrospective way. Of this data set, males were sampled who worked on the first of January of one of the years between 1985 and 1991. At the moment of sampling, the elapsed job and residence duration was asked. Workers are followed over time either until they leave the current job or until December 1991. In the case that a worker leaves the job before December 1991, he may be re-sampled at the first of January of one of the following years. So, we follow these workers for maximum of seven years. Furthermore, we restrict the sample to those who work more than 20 hours of for whom all relevant data were observed. The focus on males separate from females seems sensible, as labour market behaviour differs strongly between males and females, which manifests itself in differences in their commuting behaviour (White, 1986). The data set allows us to distinguish between voluntary and involuntary job moves due to firing. Precise information about commuting distance and commuting time is missing in our data set, as only the municipality of residence and workplace of the worker is available. So, we approximate

approximate commuting costs by the variable logarithm of the distance between the centres of the municipalities plus one.[4] The mean commuting distance is about 20 kilometres. About 40% of the persons work in the same municipality as they live. For these persons, we have fixed the commuting distance equal to zero.[5] For another analysis of the same data set, addressing related issues, in particular the differences between males and females, we refer to Camstra (1994). We include here as relevant explanatory variables those suggested by economic theory. Our choice of the explanatory variables to characterise the differences in job and residential mobility is discussed below.

Job Mobility

Job-to-job mobility is defined as a *voluntary* change of employer (which may or may not change the workplace location). Job-to-job mobility probably tends to increase with higher educational achievement, because higher education offers more opportunities to grow and more variation in wages. So, education is thought to be a form of investment which increases the return on the hours worked and offers more opportunities for an upward career (vertical job mobility).[6] The following five levels of education are included in our model: university education, polytechnic education, vocational education, low vocational education and high school. The individuals having only primary school are in the reference group.

Not only formal education, but also on-the-job experience and personal skills determine the level of relevant skills for a job. The level of skills of an individual is reflected in the position within the firm, which influences job mobility in similar way as formal education. In addition, hiring and firing costs will depend on the position of the employee within the firm, which will affect job mobility. Two different levels of positions are incorporated in the model: one group consists of employees without subordinates, the other group consists of employees with at least 4 subordinates. The reference group consists of employees with at least, but less than 4 subordinates.

It is often argued that age has an effect on the probability to leave a job, because young people are more willing to move, as they have more opportunities to grow. We have included a dummy for respondents younger than 24, for those between 24 and 34, and for those between 34 and 44; older persons are in the reference group. It is well-known that job turnover strongly fluctuates over the business cycle. For example, in the Netherlands, during the 1960s job mobility was high, while at the end of the 1970s and the beginning of the 1980s, turnover turned out to be extremely low. Instead of including a measure for the business cycle, we included dummies for groups of calendar years, which offers more flexibility. The reference year is 1991. The type of employer influences job mobility. Therefore, we included dummies for the size of the branch, whether employed in the building sector, whether employed by the government, and a dummy for those on payroll. Clearly, a high wage rate reduces the probability to leave a job voluntarily, and hence we included the (logarithm of the) hourly wage. Finally, we included a dummy for jobs with more than 32 hours.

Residential Mobility

A residential move will be observed, if the gain in place utility of the move is higher than the discounted moving costs (taking into account future moves). One may expect that some variables influence particularly the direct place utility of a residence (in particular commuting distance), while others will more likely influence the moving costs (e.g. the presence of children, tenure of dwelling). Clearly, the place utility attached by the inhabitant to the dwelling depends on characteristics which change over time (Linneman and Graves, 1983).

It is well-known that residential mobility strongly depends on the stage in the life cycle. In general, younger people experience more moves. According to the search model, this is due to a combination of lower residential moving costs, more opportunities to get a better residence offer, and higher corresponding job mobility rates. Moreover, younger people experience more changes due to marriage and divorce, therefore we have included a dummy for respondents younger than 24, between 26 and 34, and between 34 and 44. Persons above 44 are in the reference group.

The residential moving costs depend strongly on the size of the dwelling. So, we included a dummy for those who occupy houses which are not shared with other members of the household ('complete house'), and for those who have less than 4 rooms. It goes without saying that the markets for rented and owned residences differ strongly. For the renters higher mobility rates are expected as the moving costs are lower. We have included a dummy for owners. The presence of children probably increases the cost of moving, and therefore decreases the probability to move, and therefore we have included a dummy for children at home. Moreover, we suppose that the moving rates are different for those who live with their parents, with their spouse or alone.

The supply side of the Dutch housing market is extremely regulated: in the Netherlands, 95% of all rented residences are subject to a form of price regulation, while 75% of all new houses are subsidised (Van der Schaar, 1991). The regulations outlined by the government do favour particular groups, which clearly effects the mobility behaviour of those groups. In particular, lower incomes receive housing allowance and generally have to queue for a residence, while higher incomes operate more in the private sector, which is more flexible. Thus, residence offer rates are likely lower for low income groups. In addition, we expect that their moving costs are higher. So, we include a dummy for hourly wage. Finally, we have included dummies for calendar years, with 1991 as reference year.

In Appendix 6.1, descriptive data can be found. Since we deal with a group of individuals that we follow over time, we have given the values at the moment they are observed for the first time.

Reduced Form Estimates

As a point of departure, we have separately analysed job and residential mobility. As the outcomes of the parameters of the univariate and bivariate models are very similar for the probit and duration model, we present and discuss only the estimates of the bivariate models. Subsequently, we have estimated a bivariate duration model and a probit model. For the duration model, we used the bivariate discrete masspoint mixing function.

The empirical results given the discrete masspoint mixing function can be found in Table 6.1. The results based on this specification also indicate that there is no significant sign of dependence.[7] Moreover, we find that unobserved heterogeneity is quite important in the labour market, and less important in the housing market.

Using the discrete choice observations, we found that correlation is insignificant ($\rho = 0.09$; s.e. $= 0.10$). Also using a LR test, the no correlation hypothesis could not be rejected (LR $=1.6$). In line with the results of the duration model, it appears that unobserved variables do play a more important role in the labour market. As a consequence, we may conclude from this reduced form analysis, that voluntary job-to-job and residential mobility are independent. Another result is that both types of models generate apparently very similar results.

Our empirical results further suggest that a job in the public sector, educational level, wage rate, commuting distance, tenure, working full-time and the calendar year affect significantly voluntary job-to-job mobility. In accordance with search theory, young persons and higher educated persons are more mobile, because they have more opportunities to grow. The fact that persons working in the public sector are less mobile can be due to several hypothetical factors, which all point in the same direction (e.g. more job security, loss of pension funds). Moreover, we find that the wage rate influences negatively job mobility. Part-time workers have higher job mobility rates, confirming 'that men do not, as a rule, regard these jobs as permanent' (Pissarides and Wadsworth, 1994). All these results seem to correspond to our current knowledge of the labour market. The effects of age on job mobility remain debatable. At last, the estimates of the calendar years reflect the known aggregate fluctuations in job mobility in the Netherlands.

Finally, it appears that commuting distance positively influences job mobility. We calculated that the elasticity of the expected job duration (in years) with respect to commuting distance (in kilometres) is approximately -0.15. So, as a rule of thumb, an increase of 10 kilometres in commuting distance reduces the expected job duration by approximately one and half year.

Table 6.1 Empirical estimates of coefficients for voluntary job-to-job and residential mobility

	duration model		discrete choice model	
	residential mobility	job mobility	residential mobility	job mobility
variables				
* constant	-0.95 (0.42) *	1.87 (0.52) *		
* age				
< age < 24	1.21 (0.46) *	0.41 (0.36) *	0.65 (0.19) *	0.78 (0.17) *
24 < age < 34	1.50 (0.40) *	0.81 (0.26) *	0.70 (0.15) *	0.46 (0.12) *
34 < age < 44	1.15 (0.36) *	1.12 (0.21) *	0.45 (0.15) *	0.38 (0.13) *
* size of branch				
size > 200 p		-0.92 (0.16) *		-0.17 (0.10)

Table 6.1 continued

	(1)	(2)	(3)	(4)
20 p < size < 200 p		-0.40 (0.14) *		-0.16 (0.10)
* no. of subordinates				
0		-0.34 (0.16) *		-0.06 (0.10)
1,2,3		-0.07 (0.55)		0.04 (0.12)
* no public sector		0.38 (0.08) *		0.22 (0.09) *
* on payroll		0.13 (0.90)		-0.22 (0.19)
* building sector		-0.15 (0.25)		0.00 (0.15)
* more than 32 hrs		-0.20 (0.28) *		-0.56 (0.21) *
* wage rate	0.15 (0.27)	-1.90 (0.20) *	-0.09 (0.11)	-0.78 (0.12) *
* complete house	-0.77 (0.37) *		-0.43 (0.19) *	
* less than 4 rooms	0.31 (0.33)		0.37 (0.16) *	
* children	-0.66 (0.24) *		-0.17 (0.11)	
* household situation				
with spouse	-0.46 (0.28)		-0.19 (0.13)	
with parents	-0.06 (0.24)		-0.16 (0.21)	
* owner	-1.30 (0.26) *		-0.41 (0.10)*	
* educational level				
university	-0.02 (0.26)	1.20 (0.24) *	-0.01 (0.14)	0.57 (0.14) *
polytechnic	-0.65 (0.35)	0.05 (0.31)	-0.19 (0.14)	0.33 (0.13) *
vocational	-0.14 (0.22)	-0.88 (0.29)	-0.24 (0.12)	0.00 (0.12)
high school	0.28 (0.39)	1.02 (0.26)	-0.00 (0.15)	-0.01 (0.16)
low vocational	-0.63 (0.21) *	-0.38 (0.30)	-0.35 (0.12) *	-0.35 (0.13) *
* commuting d.	0.16 (0.05) *	0.09 (0.04) *	0.06 (0.02) *	0.05 (0.02) **
* calendar year				
1985/1986	0.19 (0.46)	-0.44 (0.28) *	0.20 (0.13)	-0.27 (0.12) *
1987/1988	0.39 (0.43)	-0.04 (0.16)	0.30 (0.13) *	-0.10 (0.12)
1989/1990	0.45 (0.44)	0.17 (0.29)	0.24 (0.13)	-0.03 (0.12)

* variance of individual specific heterogeneity

	(3)	(4)
σ^2	0.10 (0.12)	0.25 (0.08) *

* masspoints and probabilities

v_{11}	0.03	(0.00) *
v_{12}	0.12	(0.04) *
v_{21}	4.13	(1.99) *
v_{22}	5.58	(2.01) *
P_1	0.96	(0.01)
P_2	0.03	(0.01)
P_3	0.01	(0.01)

Table 6.1 continued

* correlation	0.03	(0.20)	0.09	(0.10)
* Loglikelihood	-1,321.26		-1,392.33	

standard errors in parentheses; *: significant at 5%.

Also the results for the residential mobility are plausible. All signs point at the expected direction. Young persons move more frequently than older persons, while also the type of the house has significant influence, probably due to differences in moving costs: owners move less, while persons in residences with less then 4 rooms and persons who live in houses which are incomplete (no own kitchen, or shower) move less. We do not find any effect whether the individual lives with his parents, alone or with a spouse. The effects for educational level are as expected; however, the wage level appears to be insignificant. The effect found for the calendar years corresponds also nicely to the aggregate fluctuations in residential mobility in the Netherlands. It appears that commuting distance positively influences residential mobility. The elasticity of the expected residence duration (in years) with respect to commuting distance (in kilometres) is almost -0.10. So, a similar rule of thumb as applied for job mobility can be used: an increase of 10 kilometres in commuting distance reduces the expected residence duration by approximately one year.

The elasticity of the expected duration of the current combination of job and residence location is estimated to be approximately -0.25, so an increase of 10 kilometres in commuting distance reduces the expected duration of the current job and residence by more than two years.

The current empirical specification relies on the assumption that housing characteristics affect only residence mobility, and that job characteristics affect only job mobility. However, according to the search model, the explanatory variables should be the same. Therefore, we have re-estimated the univariate models including the full range of explanatory variables. It appears that none of the residential characteristics affects job mobility and none of the job mobility characteristics affects residence mobility.

Finally, we have assumed that the commuting distance affects mobility, in line with the search model. Linneman and Graves (1983) hypothesise however that changes in characteristics affect residential and job mobility. We have therefore re-estimated the model including a regressor which measures the change in the commuting distance during the previous year (ignoring the data during the year when this change is unknown). The effect of this regressor appears to be highly insignificant. Furthermore, we have re-estimated the model including regressor which indicates whether the commuting distance has increased, stayed the same or has decreased during the previous year. This regressor affects job mobility positively, but the coefficient is only significant at the 10% significance level. The effect of this regressor on residential mobility was negligible. Given these specifications, the effect of the level of commuting distance was positive and significant. In conclusion, it appears that the level of the commuting distance, but not the change in the commuting distance, affect job and residential mobility.

Structural Estimates

According to search U.K., it is thought that job and residence relocations are both a result from a lifetime utility maximisation process, neither is a direct determinant of the other. Rather, they both respond to opportunities and changes in the housing and labour markets. If the explanatory variables do a good job of describing moving processes, there wouldn't be any residual relationship between job and residence relocations.

We estimated therefore a structural simultaneous probit model, by using the predicted value of a job move as a regressor in the equation for a residential move and the other way round (Zax, 1991). It appears that job moves do not influence residential mobility (β =0.18, s.e. =0.14, LR = 1.3) and residential moves do not significantly influence job mobility (β = -0.05, s.d. = 0.13, LR = 0.1). As far as we know, structural parameters cannot be estimated by means of duration models. In conclusion, we do not find any evidence that job and residential moves are mutually related (conditional on the regressors used).

So, the hypothesis that the probability to move job (residence) influences the probability to move residence (job) is rejected. However, there might be a good reason why our model does not reject the independence hypothesis even when it does not hold. Statistical models do not predict very well residential or job mobility. So, the regressors which correspond to the predicted probability of moving job or residential are poor approximations. Thus, we examine the independence hypothesis under stronger assumptions, which might eliminate this scepticism.

Stronger Assumptions About Causality: Job Moves Trigger Residential Moves

The theoretical search framework discussed in section 2 is very general. Let us make now the more restrictive, but reasonable, assumption that the probability of receiving a job offer is much smaller than the probability of receiving a residence offer. It can be shown then that it is rational for the individual firstly to move a job and then to move residence. This occurs because after a job move that increases commuting costs, the probability that the commuting costs can be reduced by moving residence is high. However, given a residential move that increases reducing commuting costs, the probability of reducing the commuting costs by moving job is small within a reasonable period. So, there are sound theoretical reasons to expect that - unconditional on commuting costs - job moves trigger residential moves, but not the other way round. In principle, the search model predicts that conditional on commuting costs this effect disappears, but it allows us to treat the observed job moves as if they were exogenous, addressing the criticism stated above that the predicted job move is not a good predictor of observed job moves. To test this result, we included a dummy of *observed* job moves as an exogenous regressor to explain residential mobility. It was found that the additional regressor was positive, but not significant at the 5% level (duration model: $\beta=0.26$, s.e$=0.14$, LR$=2.5$; discrete choice model: $\beta=0.18$, s.e. $= 0.11$, LR$= 2.9$). So, we may conclude that job moves do not strongly trigger residential moves.

Concluding Remarks

We have argued in this chapter that the relationship between job-to-job and residential mobility depends on the geographical structure of the economy. We started from a search model which assumes that workers search simultaneously on the labour and housing market, while taking into account commuting costs as well as moving costs and that they move more than once in the future. We have illustrated that such a search model is useful to understand commuting behaviour and the relationship between intra-regional and inter-regional moves.

A prediction of the search model is that job and residential mobility increase with commuting distance. We examined this result by employing a bivariate duration and a bivariate probit model. Our results show that an increase of 10 kilometres in commuting distance reduces the expected duration of the stay in the same job and residence with more than two years.

Notes

[1] For notational convenience, we do not distinguish between the observed explanatory variables x which affect t_1 and those which affect t_2.

[2] Moreover, in practice, there appears to be a trade-off between the specification of duration-dependency and the mixing function (Lancaster, 1990). When one does not allow for duration-dependency, in the empirical specification, the effect of unobserved variables on the hazard rate are generally more pronounced. Since we will investigate the hypothesis that the unobserved variables affecting job mobility are not related to the unobserved variables affecting residential mobility, we reduce the risk of not rejecting the null hypothesis.

[3] Van den Berg, Lindeboom and Ridder (1994) report that the use of more masspoints hardly changes the results. Since the results for the duration model are consistent with those from the discrete choice model, we have not attempted to estimate a more cumbersome bivariate duration model with more than four masspoints.

[4] We take the logarithm of the distance, since the marginal effect of the distance on the commuting costs will be lower when commuting distances increase. We add one, to avoid problems with commuting distances which are equal to zero. Analyses with a linear function of commuting distance give very similar results.

[5] To test whether this way of measuring commuting distance affects our results, we have re-estimated the model including a dummy for those who work in the same municipality as they live. This dummy appears to be insignificant. However, as anticipated, the coefficients of commuting distance indicate then a stronger relationship between commuting distance and mobility then reported in the current paper.

[6] Horizontal job mobility decreases with education according to the dual labour market theory (Doeringer and Piore, 1971; Mekkelholt, 1993). For example, lowly educated individuals operate more frequently in a market with temporal contracts than higher educated people. However, horizontal mobility is frequently involuntary, and workers with temporal contracts have higher probabilities of becoming unemployed.

[7] We also tested for correlation by regressing the generalised residuals of job mobility on the generalised residuals of residential mobility, which showed a positive, but insignificant relationship. For a discussion on generalised residuals, see Lancaster (1990).

Appendix 6.1 Means of variables of employed individuals

* elapsed duration
    job duration (in years)   6.62
    residence duration (in years)   8.92
* age
    < age < 24   0.17
    24 < age < 34   0.44
    34 < age < 44   0.23
* size of branch
    size > 200 p   0.34
    20 p < size < 200 p   0.32
* number of subordinates
    0   0.18
    > 3   0.12
* no public sector   0.65
* on payroll   0.95
* building sector   0.07
* more than 32 hours   0.96
* logarithm of wage rate   2.79
* 'complete house'   0.74
* less than 4 rooms   0.05
* children   0.30
* household situation
    with spouse   0.66
    with parents   0.21
* owner   0.34
* educational level
    university   0.12
    polytechnic   0.16
    vocational   0.23
    high school   0.07
    low vocational   0.23
* commuting distance   20.06
* calendar year
    1985/1986   0.78
    1987/1988   0.09
    1989/1990   0.08

7. Willingness to Pay for Commuting

Introduction

In the current chapter, we will propose a new method to estimate the marginal willingness of workers to pay (MWP) for commuting. There has been in general interest in this topic (see, for example, Van den Berg and Gorter, 1997). Information on the willingness of workers to pay in order to avoid additional commuting might help to evaluate policy measures directed to the abatement of commuting. For example, the direct cost of an additional minute commuting due to increased congestion can be calculated.

The marginal willingness of workers to pay for job attributes can be estimated using static hedonic price methods (see Rosen, 1974). Recently, Gronberg and Reed (1994) have proposed a method to estimate the willingness to pay for fixed job attributes based on job moving behaviour. In this chapter, we will extend their method by showing how one may estimate workers' marginal willingness to pay for nonwage characteristics which are not fixed to the job (e.g. commuting distance). The existence of nonwage characteristics which can be varied seems quite common. Several examples can be given. For example, commuting distance may be reduced by moving residence closer to the job, some unpleasant characteristics of a job might be removed by complaining about them, or joining an union might decrease the probability of being fired.

In the current chapter, estimates for workers' marginal willingness to pay for commuting are obtained by using information on job duration data and *voluntary* transitions and by making use of the job and residence search model introduced in Chapter 3.

The Marginal Willingness to Pay for Commuting

In Chapter 3, we have introduced a search model which describes the behaviour of a worker who searches for jobs and residences. We will show that the marginal willingness to pay for commuting can be derived based upon the job acceptance rule and the first-order condition for the optimal reservation wage. For those who are employed we have obtained in Chapter 3 the following job acceptance rule:

Given a job offer of wage w_y and commuting distance z_y, and given the wage w, place utility r, commuting distance z, and reservation wage $res_w(w,r,z|z_y)$:

change job   if $w_y > res_w(w,r,z|z_y)$

otherwise do not change job.

The optimal reservation wage is characterised by the following first-order condition (see Chapter 3):

$$V(res_w(w,r,z\,|\,z_y),r,z_y) = V(w,r,z) + c_1$$

where $V(w,r,z)$ is the lifetime utility of a job with characteristics w, r and z, and c_1 are the job moving costs.

The marginal willingness to pay for a job characteristic may be defined as the amount wage the worker is willing to pay for an additional unit of the job characteristic. So the workers' marginal willingness to pay for commuting distance z is defined by

$$MWP(z) = \frac{\dfrac{\partial V(w,r,z)}{\partial z}}{\dfrac{\partial V(w,r,z)}{\partial w}}$$

In words, the marginal willingness to pay for commuting distance z equals the ratio of the marginal change in lifetime utility V due to a marginal increase in z and the marginal change in lifetime utility V due to a marginal increase in the wage.

Given the bivariate wage and commuting distance density function $f_{wz}(x,y)$ and the job arrival rate p_1, the voluntary job-to-job hazard rate function $\theta_w(w,r,z)$ is defined as:

$$\theta_w(w,r,z) = p_1 \int_0^{\bar{z}} \int_{res_w(w,r,z|y)}^{\bar{w}} f(x,y)dxdy$$

Accordingly, $V(w,r,z)$ and $\theta_w(w,r,z)$ both depend on w and z via $res_w(w,r,z|z_y)$. As a consequence,

$$MWP(z) = \frac{\dfrac{\partial \theta_w(w,r,z)}{\partial z}}{\dfrac{\partial \theta_w(w,r,z)}{\partial w}}$$

Consequently, the worker's MWP for commuting distance is equal to the ratio of the marginal effect of commuting distance on the job-to-job hazard function and the marginal effect of the wage on the job-to-job hazard function.[1]

Estimation

An implication of the previous result is that one may estimate of the marginal willingness of worker's to pay for job characteristics requires the statistical analysis of job duration data. Our aim is to estimate $(\partial \theta_w/\partial z) / (\partial \theta_w/\partial w)$, i.e. the ratio of the marginal effects of commuting distance and the wage on the job-to-job hazard function. For example, suppose that the hazard function belongs to the class of Mixed Proportional Hazard models:

$$\theta_w(X,t,v) = \lambda(t) \cdot \exp(\beta_w \cdot w + \beta_z \cdot z + X\beta) \cdot v,$$

where the baseline-hazard $\lambda(t)$ is a function of t which captures the time-dependencies in the hazard function, X consists of all observed variables expect w and z and v is an random variable independent of the observable variables. Given estimates of β_w and β_z, the ratio of the marginal effects of commuting distance and the wage on the hazard function θ_w can be easily calculated as

$$(\partial\theta_w/\partial z) / (\partial\theta_w/\partial w) = \beta_z / \beta_w.$$

Of course, also other assumptions on the functional form of θ_w can be made. In the empirical part of this study, we suppose that θ_w is a function in logarithms of w and z. As a consequence,

$$(\partial\theta_w/\partial z) / (\partial\theta_w/\partial w) = (\beta_z / \beta_w) * w / z.$$

An Empirical Application

In the previous chapter, we have estimated β_z and β_w. The implied MWP(z) evaluated at an average distance of 20 kilometres and a net wage of 20 guilder per hours equals about -0.04, with a standard error of 0.02.[2] As a consequence, the MWP(z) for an additional kilometre per working day of 8 hours is estimated to be about -0.32.[3] The MWP for commuting distance implies a MWP for commuting time. Based on the EBB (1992), we calculate the average commuting speed which depends on the mode used. According to the EBB (1992), commuters who use the car travel with an average speed of about 32 kilometres per hour for commutes of less than 16 kilometres. Commuters who travel by more than 16 kilometres travel on average twice as fast. Based on these figures, the marginal value of commuting time (including expenses) is about 1/3 of the wage for the first half hour; for those who commute more than a half hour, the marginal value of time is about 2/3. These empirical findings are in line with other empirical studies (see Small, 1992). For slower means of transport (e.g. the bicycle) the implied marginal value of commuting time is lower.[4]

Conclusion

This chapter contributes to the literature by showing that the method to estimate the marginal willingness to pay for non-fixed variables like commuting can be easily applied given information on job duration data and voluntary transitions.

Our estimates imply that the marginal willingness to pay to avoid additional commuting time for workers who commute more than a half hour by car or train is about 2/3, whereas for those who commute less than a half hour we find values around 1/3.

Notes

[1] In case that z is fixed to the job, the MWP(z) equals $(\partial v / \partial z)$ / $(\partial v / \partial w)$ where v denotes the instantaneous utility function. This result was also obtained by Gronberg and Reed (1994). In this more restricted case, MWP(z) does not depend on any other parameter in the model, so the estimates are structural.

[2] The standard error is calculated using the delta method.

[3] We have also compared the empirical estimates using duration data with the conventional hedonic wage method. Hwang, Reed and Hubbard (1993) demonstrate that conventional estimates of the marginal willingness to pay for a desirable characteristics by using hedonic wage methods are biased down within a framework of an equilibrium model of job search. Employing simulation data derived from an equilibrium search model, Gronberg and Reed (1994) conclude that the MWP estimates from the hedonic wage method are seriously downward biased. Gronberg and Reed (1994) also compare the empirical MWP estimates from the job duration model with the empirical MWP estimates from the hedonic wage method, and find the conventional MWP are biased much lower. Employing the hedonic wage method, we find that the marginal willingness to pay for commuting is about 1/2 of the MWP estimate based on duration data.

[4] The reason for this is that workers realise that commuting costs are temporary as they may move job or residence in the future.

8. Job Moving Behaviour: Impacts of Employed Spouses

Introduction

In this chapter, we intend to investigate whether the job moving behaviour of workers who belong to a two-earner household behave structurally different from single wage-earners' job moving behaviour. Two-earner households consist of two wage earners who have different working places, but share a dwelling, which restricts the choice set of acceptable jobs. Using search theory, we have hypothesised therefore that workers belonging to a two-earner household move job less often than single wage-earners. Furthermore, we have hypothesised that the spouse's workplace location would affect job. However, it may be argued that workers belonging to a two-earner household will move more often. For example, the presence of a spouse may reduce the risks involved with moving job (for example, loss of tenure), since the spouse contributes to the household income. This would imply that job mobility does not depend on spouse's workplace location, but on the spouse's wage. Plausibly, these effects are stronger for female than for male workers, since male spouses are less likely to leave the labour market. Empirical investigations of the consequence of an employed spouse on job mobility are unknown to us. Previous job mobility studies sometimes include information on the presence of spouse, but generally not the presence of a *working* spouse. For example, Viscusi (1980) reports that married workers move less than single individuals.

The practical importance of emphasising the presence of employed spouses is evident from the large share of wage earners who belong to two-earner households. For example, in the Netherlands, about one third of employed persons is currently part of a two-earner household (EBB, 1992), whereas in most other developed countries this share is even significantly higher. Also for policy purposes this analysis is relevant. If it is true that two-earner households are less flexible on the housing and labour market, an increase in the share of two-earner households would mean that the average commuter will become less sensitive to transport policy measures aiming at reducing commuting distances.

Although the impacts of employed spouses on job behaviour have been ignored in the job mobility literature, these impacts have been examined in the migration literature (see, among others, Sandell, 1977; Graves and Linneman, 1977; Linneman and Graves, 1983; or for a more recent contribution, Opek and Merrill, 1997). It is therefore relevant to make a distinction between migration and other types of job mobility (see Roseman, 1971). Migration typically involves a job and residence move over a long distance, so the household leaves the local labour market and living environment. Since almost all job and residential moves are over short distances, the number of moves that may be interpreted as a migration is low.[1] As a consequence, results obtained on the moving behaviour of two-earner households based on the analysis of data behaviour cannot be generalised to the moving behaviour of two-earner households in general. In the context of the effect of an employed spouse on mobility, theories about migration are different from those which deal with all types of moves. A migration of a worker implies always a residential move of the whole household. However, a job move does not necessarily have the same implications.

Although the conclusion obtained by means of an empirical analysis of migration of two-earner households cannot be generalised to the job moving behaviour of two-earner households, in general the results obtained for migration moves indicate that the same result may hold for job moving behaviour. For example, it is well known that single individuals *migrate* more frequently than married individuals (Mincer, 1978). Similarly, the likelihood of a family migration is reduced when the wife of the employee is employed (Sandell, 1977). This suggests, but certainly does not imply, that single individuals move job more frequently than those who have an employed spouse or are married.

In the job moving and migration literature, it has been found that certain job characteristics of the spouse (for example, the spouse's job tenure) have a strong effect on the job moving likelihood. The effect of the spatial location of the spouse's job has been ignored, although we have seen that there are theoretical reasons to expect that job mobility depends on the spatial location of the spouse's job (see chapter 4). As far as we know this issue has not been empirically investigated.

In summary, in this chapter we will examine the determinants of job mobility for single wage-earners (with and without spouse) and two-earner households. Our empirical analysis will again be based on a hazard model. We aim to test the hypothesis that on-the-job moving behaviour differs for two-earner households and single wage-earners. Moreover, we examine whether job moving behaviour depends on the spatial location of the spouse's job.

The structure of this chapter is as follows. First, the data are discussed. The next section contains the empirical results, a discussion of these results and an examination of the robustness of the results regarding the model specification chosen. The final section offers concluding remarks.

The Data and the Explanatory Variables

The Data

The Telepanel data set is used again, it is collected in 1992-1993, includes the complete life course pattern of about 3000 Dutch respondents, including the labour career. The data were collected in a retrospective way. The data set allows for a distinction between voluntary moves and involuntary job moves (due to firing).[2] From this data set, we have selected 589 persons who worked at least 20 hours per week in the period between 1985 and 1991 and for which all relevant data are observed. A household that consists of two wage earners of whom one works at least 32 hours per week (and the other one at least 20 hours) is defined to be a two-earner household.[3] 122 observations refer to workers who are part of a two-earner household.[4] We follow the households over time between January 1985 and December 1991 and observe the job duration. After a job move, the household continues to be included in the analysis, so we have multiple job duration observations.

The Explanatory Variables

In the empirical analysis, we have used a large number of explanatory variables (for a more extensive description of some variables see chapter 6). We discuss these variables here. The following levels of education are included: university, polytechnic, vocational, high school, low vocational. Individuals only having primary school are in the reference group. Job-to-job mobility is thought to increase with higher educational achievement, because higher education offers a higher career potential. Not only formal education, but also the position within the firm affects mobility: we include therefore the number of subordinates and whether the persons works more than 32 hours per week.

We include the size of the branch. Size of branch is defined as the number of persons working at the same workplace location of the firm. This variable is a proxy for the size of the firm. It is generally thought that larger firms offer more opportunities to grow within the firm and offer better employment conditions which reduce workers' job mobility. It is generally thought that those who work as a civil servant will move less, so we include also a dummy to capture such an effect.

Calendar year effects are incorporated to capture changes in general labour market conditions by including bi-annual dummies. In addition, the logarithm of wage rate is included, since a higher wage reduces job mobility (it is common to use the logarithm of the wage instead of the wage in job mobility studies, see for example Van den Berg, 1992, 1995).

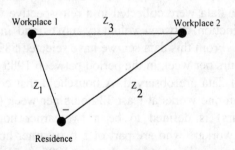

Figure 8.1 The workplace and residential locations of a two-earner household.

Furthermore, we include a range of individual and household explanatory variables:[5] a dummy for the presence of a spouse and a dummy whether the spouse is employed (two-earner household), the ratio of the worker's wage over the spouse's wage, a dummy for males, dummies for age groups, and a dummy for the presence of children. Furthermore, the dummy for the presence of a spouse, the dummy for the two-earner household, the dummy for the presence of children are gender-dependent. The time-varying variables are allowed to differ yearly.

We include also information on the commuting distance, z_1, and the commuting distance of the spouse, z_2 (see Figure 8.1). We hypothesise that the effect of commuting distance z_1 on job mobility is positive. The effect of the spouse's commuting distance z_2 is ambiguous (see chapter 4). Our explanation for this ambiguity is the following: given an increase in z_2, the household is more likely to move residence. This gives the worker an incentive to accept less job offers close to the current residential location *and* an incentive to accept more job offers far from the current residential location. As a result, the effect of z_2 on job mobility is ambiguous. Nevertheless, we hypothesise that it is likely that the overall effect is positive, since the probability of receiving a job offer at a distance which is longer than the current distance is for most workers larger then the probability of receiving a job offer at a distance which is shorter than the current distance. For example, suppose that employment is uniformly distributed over space: $g(z_1) = c.2.\pi.z_1$ for $z_1 < z_{max}$, where the density $g(z_1)$ denotes the distribution of commuting distance offers, z_{max} is the maximum value of z_1 and c is a normalisation constant. Let us consider a worker of whom the current commuting distance is 1/5 of the maximum commuting distance offered.[6] The probability that an at random job offer will reduce the current commuting distance is 0.04. As a consequence, the probability that an at random job offer will increase the current commuting distance is 0.96.

In the data set, exact information about the commuting distance is missing, as only data on the municipalities of residence and workplace of the individuals are available. We approximate commuting distance by the distance between the centres of the municipalities (measured in kilometres).[7] We also include the distance between the workplaces z_3 (see Figure 8.1). Theoretical reasoning suggests the effect of z_3 on job mobility to be positive.

We may explain the effect of z_3 as follows (see chapter 4). For smaller values of z_3, the household is maximally able to reduce the commuting distances of both spouses by means of a residential move. This can be easily understood as follows. Suppose that z_3 is zero and therefore both wage earners work at the same location. In this situation, *any* residential move that reduces z_1 will also reduce z_2, which will make a residential move *more* attractive. As an alternative, suppose that z_3 is equal to the sum of z_1 and z_2, so the residence location is exactly between the two job locations. In this situation, *any* residential move that reduces z_1 will simultaneously increase z_2, which makes moving residence *less* attractive. So, more generally, the household is better off given smaller values of z_3, and the household has therefore an incentive to reduce z_3 by means of a job move. Consequently, we hypothesise that for larger values of z_3, two-earner households will move job more frequently.

The Empirical Results

The Estimates

The empirical results of the hazard coefficients can be found in Table 8.1, model I.[8] First, we will discuss the variables that are related to the distinction between two-earner households and single wage-earners.

The results appear to indicate that the effect of the presence of a spouse (employed or not) are not significant generally using a significance level of 5%. However, a closer look at the results shows that the coefficient for *females who belong to a two-earner household* is significant and equals -1.02. The latter effect has been calculated as the sum of the estimated coefficients of the dummies for a two-earner, a spouse, two-earner (if female) and spouse (if female). Note that these dummies do not exclude each other. The variance of this estimate equals 0.32 (see Appendix 8.1). Thus, female wage earners who belong to a two-earner household have a significantly lower job mobility than single wage-earners.

As explained in the introduction, a plausible explanation for this effect is that female workers who belong to a two-earner household are less flexible in the housing market, since they take the workplace location of their spouses into account, and thus will not accept job offers from employers at a large distance of the current residence.[9] As a consequence, female members of two-earner households may be less able than single wage-earners to obtain jobs that pay higher wages.

Similarly, it appears that the coefficient for *females who have a spouse* is significant and equals -0.75 (the standard error is 0.32, for details see Appendix 8.1). Thus, female wage earners with a spouse (employed or not) have a lower job mobility than single wage-earners.

A comparison of *female* workers who belong to a two-earner household with *male* workers who belong to two-earner household, indicates that females move less, although the effect is only significant at the 10% significance level (the effect is -0.70 and the standard error is 0.37).

It is important to notice that, according to our results, on-the-job moving behaviour of a female worker does depend on the presence of a spouse, but the effect is stronger given the presence of an *employed* spouse. Hence, we find that belonging to a two-earner household and the presence of a spouse (employed or not) reduce *females'* on-the-job moving behaviour. As a consequence, many females may reject job offers which are accepted by male workers. This finding contributes to our understanding why the wage growth of female workers is less than that of male workers (Sandell, 1977; Loprest, 1992).

The empirical results provide evidence that the spatial location of the spouse's job affects job moving behaviour. In particular, we find that the spouse's commuting distance z_2 increases job mobility. Such a result is in line with our hypothesis. However, the empirical results do not indicate that the effect of z_3 on job mobility is positive. Consequently, we do not find empirical support for our hypothesis that for larger values of z_3, two-earner households will move job more frequently.

Table 8.1 Empirical coefficients for hazard rates for leaving job voluntarily (a)

variables (b)	model I	model II	model III	model IV
	all observations	all observations	with spouse	two-earner
* Two-earner	-0.12	-0.11	-0.59	
	(0.29)	(0.29)	(0.28)*	
* Spouse	-0.20	-0.20		
	(0.19)	(0.18)		
* Two-earner (if female)	-0.15	-0.15	0.15	
	(0.38)	(0.38)	(0.47)	
* Spouse (if female)	-0.55	-0.55		
	(0.37)	(0.38)		
* Children (if female)	0.49	0.48	0.15	0.86
	(0.30)	(0.31)	(0.47)	(0.47)
* Workplace location of the spouse:				
commuting distance z_2	0.14	0.11	0.10	0.13
	(0.06) *	(0.07)	(0.10)	(0.05)*
α (in radians)		0.19		
		(0.14)		
z_3 (d)	-0.01		-0.02	0.00
	(0.09)		(0.10)	(0.12)

Table 8.1 continued

* Commuting distance z_1 (d)	0.47	0.46	0.64	1.88
	(0.24) *	(0.28)	(0.25) *	(0.62) *
* Wage rate (c)	-2.19	-2.23	-1.05	-1.26
	(0.19) *	(0.20) *	(0.23) *	(0.66)
* Wage / wage of spouse	0.01	0.01		
	(0.02)	(0.02)		
* Male	1.41	1.40	1.01	0.55
	(0.64) *	(0.62) *	(0.60)	(0.39)
* Age				
< age < 24	0.76	0.76	1.21	2.66
	(0.29) *	(0.29) *	(0.52) *	(1.06) *
24 < age < 34	0.70	0.69	1.11	1.75
	(0.25) *	(0.25) *	(0.49) *	(0.99)
34 < age < 44	0.95	0.94	1.10	1.51
	(0.22) *	(0.22) *	(0.50) *	(1.00)
* Size of branch				
size > 200 p	-0.75	-0.76		-0.48
	(0.15) *	(0.15) *		(0.45)
20 p < size < 200 p	-0.44	-0.44		-0.48
	(0.12) *	(0.12) *		(0.37)
* More than 32 working hours	-0.13	-0.13		-0.87
	(0.18)	(0.18)		(0.47)
* Number of subordinates				
0	0.13	0.13		-0.42
	(0.18)	(0.18)		(0.56)
1,2,3	-0.13	-0.12		0.40
	(0.19)	(0.19)		(0.51)
* No civil servant	-0.01	-0.01		
	(0.06)	(0.06)		
* Educational level				
university	0.87	0.88	0.78	1.06
	(0.27) *	(0.27) *	(0.30) *	(0.53)*
polytechnic	0.08	0.08	0.06	
	(0.18)	(0.18)	(0.23)	
vocational	-0.52	-0.52	-0.44	
	(0.19) *	(0.19) *	(0.19) *	
high school	0.35	0.31	-0.01	
	(0.24)	(0.25)	(0.25)	
low vocational	-0.77	-0.76	-0.33	
	(0.23) *	(0.23) *	(0.25)	

Table 8.1 continued

* Lives with parents	-0.62	-0.63		
	(0.19) *	(0.19) *		
* Children	0.18	0.18	0.47	0.14
	(0.22)	(0.22)	(0.34)	(0.32)
* Calendar year				
1985/1986	-0.65	-0.64	-0.52	
	(0.17) *	(0.17) *	(0.23) *	
1987/1988	-0.36	-0.36	-0.22	
	(0.15)	(0.15)	(0.23)	
1989/1990	-0.16	0.16	(0.01)	
	(0.15)	(0.15)	(90.15)	
* Masspoints and probabilities				
v_1	1.37	1.26	0.13	0.22
	(1.74)	(1.64)	(0.05) *	(0.61)
v_2	6.99	5.99	0.82	2.27
	(1.13) *	(1.11) *	(0.10) *	(0.88)*
P_1	0.99	0.99	0.99	0.99
	(0.01)	(0.01)	(0.01)	(0.43)
P_2	0.01	0.01	0.01	0.01
	(0.01)	(0.01)	(0.63)	(0.42)
Number of observations	589	589	420	122
Loglikelihood	-1010.61	-1011.42	-648.16	-119.69

(a) Standard errors in parentheses; *: significant at 5%.
(b) Reference groups: type of household (single wage-earner), household situation (no spouse), male (female), age (older than 44), size of branch (less than 20), more than 32 working hours (less than 32), number of subordinates (more than 3), no civil servant (civil servant), educational level (primary and unknown), calendar year (1991).
(c) Logarithm of net wage per hour (in Dutch guilders).
(d) Distance in 10 kilometres.

The results of the effects of the other explanatory variables in the model are essentially in line with previous studies of the labour market. We find that those with higher wages move less and that commuting distance positively affects job mobility. These results correspond to results, inter alia, by Zax (1991), Van den Berg (1992) and Van Ophem (1991). Furthermore, the variables age, size of the branch, number of subordinates, educational level and calendar years are found to be statistically significant.[10] These results do not need further discussion. Finally, we found that unobserved variables play a role as an explanation for the observed moving behaviour. According to the results, 2% of the workers has about 4.5 times higher hazard rates of moving job than the other workers ($v_1 = 1.37$, $v_2 = 6.99$).

The Robustness of the Estimation Results

Now we will examine whether the empirical results as presented above are sensitive concerning the model specification chosen.

Firstly, it has been assumed that the mixing distribution $h(v)$ is parameterised with two discrete masspoints. Hence, we have re-estimated the model assuming that the mixing distribution is parameterised with three discrete masspoints. It appeared that the results were essentially identical.

Secondly, we have assumed that the effect of the spatial location of the spouse's job can be measured by means of the variables z_2 and z_3. However, as an alternative, one may use z_2 and the angle between z_1 and z_2, denoted as α. Clearly, α and z_3 are positively, but non-linearly, related to each other, conditional on z_1 and z_2 (by the law of cosines, $z_3^2 = z_1^2 + z_2^2 - 2.z_1.z_2. \cos(\alpha)$, $0 < \alpha < \pi$; $\partial z_3^2 / \partial \alpha = 2.z_1.z_2.\sin(\alpha) \geq 0$). We have therefore re-estimated the model using α instead of z_3 (model II). It appeared that the effect of α is positive. Nevertheless, the results show that the effect of α is not significant at the 5% level. Given this specification, the coefficient of the 'commuting distance of the spouse' is insignificant at the 5% level.[11] Hence, although both specifications provide evidence that the spatial location of the spouse's job affects job mobility, it is not clear which factor (viz. z_2, z_3 or α) is the main cause.[12] In conclusion, we are able to provide some evidence against the null hypothesis that the spatial location of the spouse's job does not affect job mobility. Nevertheless, we fail to provide evidence how the spatial location of the spouse's job affects job mobility. More decisive results may be expected with larger data sets.

Thirdly, one may argue that single wage-earners and two-earner households behave in structurally different ways, which cannot be captured only by means of one single regressor 'two-earner household'. Therefore, the model is re-estimated on two subsets of observations. We have re-estimated the model given a subset of observations of workers who live with a spouse (who may be employed or nonemployed) and given a subset of observations of workers who live together with an *employed* spouse (model III and IV). In the latter estimations, we have restricted the range of explanatory variables, since the number of observations is limited. It appears that the estimation results do not contradict those presented above (however, since many coefficients are insignificant, the power of this test is limited). The only difference is that the results of model III indicate that job mobility is reduced by the presence of a working spouse for females as well as for males. Nevertheless, the effects of the coefficient for the explanatory variable male in model III and model IV indicate that females with a spouse and females with an employed spouse move less job, so the original conclusion that 'females who belong to a two-earner household move less job' is not invalidated. Hence, we conclude that the results presented are robust with the chosen specification.

Conclusion

We have tested the hypothesis that on-the-job moving behaviour differs for two-earner households and single wage-earners. Given a data set of two-earners and single wage-earners in the Netherlands, we found that female workers with a spouse, but particularly when they belong to a two-earner household, tend to move less job than other workers. This might be interpreted as a sign that many female workers with a spouse refuse job offers which are accepted by other workers. The empirical results indicate that job mobility does not depend strongly on the spatial location of the spouse's job.

Notes

[1] Data presented in Linneman and Graves (1983) for the US indicate that only 11% of the heads of households who changed job also changed county of residence in the same year. The percentage of moves that may be interpreted as a migration is much less, since a change of county does not necessarily imply a move over a large distance: according to the same data, 50% of the heads of households who changed county of residence did not change job in the same year. In the Netherlands the average distance between the old and the new residence is 4.2 kilometres, while 75% of all residential moves are less than 15 kilometres (van Dijk, 1986).

[2] We do not distinguish between voluntary job-to-job moves and voluntary job-to-nonemployment moves.

[3] A rationale of this definition of a two-earner household is that it is generally thought that the labour market behaviour of a worker who does not work full-time does not influence the labour market behaviour of the worker's spouse.

[4]Both wage earners of a two-earner household are among the 122 observations. So, job mobility behaviour of these workers is dependent. This type of dependency does not effect the consistency of the estimates, and is ignored here.

[5]Characteristics that are only defined for two-earner households are set to zero in the case of single wage-earners.

[6]This seems a plausible assumption for the average worker in the Netherlands. The median distance is about 10 kilometers. So, we assume that jobs are offered within a range of 50 kilometers.

[7]Since the commuting distance is observed with a potentially large measurement error, the reported effect of commuting distance is an underestimate. Furthermore, the survey does not contain information on commuting time. This is unfortunate, since commuting time has a stronger effect on job search behaviour than commuting distance has. In addition, Dubin (1991) has shown for the United States that workers react stronger to changes in commuting time than to changes in commuting distance.

[8]We assume that job moving behaviour does not differ for males and females except for a number of gender dependent dummies (see Viscusi, 1980). We have tested the hypothesis that job moving behaviour differs for males and females by estimating the models for males and females separately. The sum of the loglikelihood of these two models is about 15 higher than the models presented in the current paper. Using a standard Likelihood-Ratio test, the hypothesis that job moving behaviour differs for males and females cannot be rejected.

[9]An alternative explanation would be that single-wage earners receive more job offers than two-earner households, for example, because single-wage earners might be more productive according to the employers. The latter explanation, however, is, as far as we know, not supported by empirical facts.

[10]We have also estimated the model using annual dummies. Given this specification however, the covariance matrix, computed as the inverse of the computed Hessian, failed to invert.

[11]In addition, in model II, the coefficient of commuting distance z_1 is not significant at the 5% level. However, this coefficient seems to be less pronounced due to the collinearity of the regressors 'commuting distance' and 'commuting distance of spouse'. We have re-estimated the model excluding the regressor 'commuting distance of spouse'. The estimates were hardly affected by this exclusion, except for the coefficient of 'commuting distance' that became significant at the 5% level.

[12]To explore this result further, we have tested whether the specification that includes α, or the specification that includes z_3, is more appropriate. Since the two specifications are non-nested, a statistical 'encompassing' test of the specifications is used (Mizon and Richard, 1986). It appears that at the 5% significance level, one cannot distinguish between the two specifications (both specifications are not rejected).

Appendix 8.1 Variance of estimates

Given random variables $X_1, \ldots, X_n$, the variance of the sum of the random variables can be written as

$$\text{var}(\sum_1^n X_i) = \sum_1^n \text{var } X_i + 2\sum_i \sum_{<j} \text{cov}(X_i X_j).$$

The covariance matrix of the estimates β for 1) a spouse, 2) two-earner 3) two-earner (if female) and 4) spouse (if female) has been estimated as:

$$
\begin{bmatrix}
0.04 & & & \\
-0.02 & 0.08 & & \\
0.02 & -0.07 & 0.14 & \\
-0.04 & 0.03 & -0.07 & 0.14
\end{bmatrix}
$$

The variance of the sum of an effect can then be calculated using the above formula and the estimated covariance matrix. For example, the variance of the presence of an employed spouse for female workers is equal to 0.04 + 0.08 + 0.14 + 0.14 + 2(-0.02 + 0.02 - 0.04 - 0.07 + 0.03 - 0.07). So the standard error is equal is 0.32.

9. Job Moving Behaviour: Two-Earner Households Revisited

Introduction

We are interested here in the relationship between on-the-job mobility rates of wage earners belonging to the same household. It seems plausible that these rates are related to each other via variables that we do not observe in a data set. In particular, many housing and household characteristics are identical for workers belonging to the same household, but are not observed. A natural method is then to estimate this relationship using a bivariate duration model that allows for unobserved variables (see chapter 6). By allowing for dependency between the unobserved variables, the efficiency of the estimation method is improved. This may be of particular importance in the case of the analysis of small data sets.

Empirical Investigation

The Data

The data set used here is the same as in previous chapters, contains the complete life course pattern of about 3000 Dutch respondents, including the labour career. The data were collected in a retrospective way. The data set allows for a distinction between voluntary moves and involuntary job moves (due to firing). From this data set, we have selected 57 two-earner households for which all relevant data are observed. By construction, every two-earner household consists of two wage earners of different gender, so we observe 57 males and 57 females. These wage earners worked at least 20 hours per week in the period between 1985 and 1991. On the basis of this data set, we were able to follow these households over time between January 1985 and December 1991 and to observe the job durations of both wage earners. After a job move, the household continues to be included in the analysis, so that we have multiple job duration observations. Within the period of observation, we observe 46 job moves. In case a worker becomes non-employed or the household dissolves, the job duration is censored.

The Empirical Results

The main contribution of this chapter is to analyse job mobility of workers belonging to a two-earner household while allowing for a mutual dependence between the unobserved variables. It seems therefore useful to compare the results with analyses that either ignore unobserved variables or ignore the mutual dependence between unobserved variables. So, before we interpret the estimates based on a model using the bivariate mixing function (model III), we will present the results based on a model using a univariate mixing function (model II) and the results based on a model which excludes unobserved variables (model I). In Table 9.1, the results for model I, II and III are reported.

Let us first focus on the results of model II. It appears that the difference between the two masspoints is -2.27 with a standard error of 0.88. Hence, the two masspoints are different and one may conclude that unobserved variables do cause the workers to move job. The results indicate that about 1% of the persons have about 10 times lower hazard rates that are not explained by observed explanatory variables included in the analysis ($\exp^{-2.27} = 0.10$). The difference in the loglikelihood between model I and model II is 6.02. The value of a Likelihood Ratio test is therefore 12.04 and the hypothesis of no unobserved variables is rejected at a 1% significance level ($\chi^2(2)=9.21$). Hence, we conclude that model II, which allows for unobserved variables, is statistically superior to model I, which ignores unobserved variables.

Let us now focus on the results of model III. One of the estimated properties was practically equal to zero (smaller than 0.00001). Thus, we have therefore proceeded by fixing this probability equal to zero. The results given this assumption, can be found in Table 9.1 (model III). Given the estimates, we have also calculated the correlation between the unobserved variables.

The difference in the loglikelihood between model II and model III is 4.14. The value of a Likelihood Ratio test is therefore 8.28 and the validity of the model II is rejected at a 1% significance level ($\chi^2(1)=6.63$). Hence, we conclude that the model that allows for the mutual dependence between the unobserved variables is statistically superior to the model that ignores this dependence. Interesting enough, the correlation between the unobserved variables appears to be highly insignificant and is equal to 0.01. The finding of no correlation seems a puzzle to us in the light of the finding that model III is statistically superior to model II. See, for a similar finding however, Butler, Anderson and Burkhauser (1989).

As can be seem from Table 9.1, the model that allows for mutual dependence between the unobserved variables does not give substantially different results for the coefficients of the explanatory variables when compared to the models which ignore this dependence (compare the results of model I, II and III in Table 9.1). However, the estimated effects of the explanatory variables on job mobility are sometimes changed and the estimates are more precisely estimated when using model III. In particular, the coefficients of the explanatory variables size of the branch, the number of subordinates, commuting distance and full-time employed appear to be significant according to model III, whereas model I fails to pick up these effects.

In conclusion, we find that the use of a bivariate mixing distribution does not change the results fundamentally. However, the precision of the estimates is improved, which might be consequential for the analysis. For similar conclusions, see the studies of Butler, Anderson and Burkhauser (1989) and Van den Berg, Lindeboom and Ridder (1996).

We have shown before that the marginal willingness to pay for commuting can be derived from duration data on job mobility. In case it is assumed that the *logarithm* of the wage determines job mobility, it can be shown that the marginal willingness to pay for commuting distance as a percentage of the wage equals $0.01*\beta_d/\beta_w$, whereas β_d is the coefficient of the commuting distance and β_w the coefficient of the wage. Hence, the marginal willingness to pay for commuting distance is proportional to the current wage.

According to model I, the marginal willingness to pay for commuting distance (measured in 10 kilometres, one-way) is -0.88% of the hourly wage, whereas its standard error is 0.83%. According to model II, the marginal willingness to pay for commuting distance is -1.23%, whereas its standard error is 0.55%. According to model III, the marginal willingness to pay for commuting distance is equal to -1.22%, whereas its standard error is 0.54%. Thus, according model II and III, the willingness to pay for commuting is significant at a 5% significance level. Note that the marginal willingness to pay for commuting distance is negative, so one should interpret these results as the marginal willingness to pay to *avoid* commuting distance.

Assuming that a person works for eight hours a day and travels at a speed of 30 kilometres per hour in both directions, this implies that the marginal willingness to pay for the absence of commuting *time* is about 146% of the hourly wage and its standard error is 66%. This percentage is considerably higher than those reported by other studies that generally find estimates of less than 100% and usually around 30-40% (see Small, 1992).

Note however that it is not implausible that a wage earner belonging to a two-earner household has a higher marginal willingness to pay for commuting time than a single wage-earner, since the latter worker is more flexible regarding a residential move and will be able to reduce the commuting time by means of a residential move. Finally, although the estimates of the marginal willingness to pay for commuting time are higher than previous estimates, we are not able to reject the hypothesis that the marginal willingness to pay for commuting time is different from the conventional levels at the 5% significance level.

Table 9.1 Empirical Coefficients for Hazard Rates for Leaving Job [a]

variables [b]	model I		model II		model III	
< age < 24	3.74	(1.17)	3.78	(1.17)	2.47	(0.73)
24 < age < 34	2.77	(1.08)	3.36	(1.11)	2.02	(0.56)
34 < age < 44	2.25	(1.07)	3.09	(1.13)	1.80	(0.45)
* Size of branch						
size > 200 p	-0.48	(0.46)	-0.92	(0.40)	-1.50	(0.38)
20 p < size < 200 p	-0.48	(0.38)	-0.83	(0.35)	-1.61	(0.34)
* Number of subordinates						
0	-0.43	(0.56)	-1.38	(0.59)	-0.23	(0.33)
1, 2, 3	0.40	(0.52)	0.31	(0.46)	0.58	(0.35)
* Commuting d.[d]	0.10	(0.07)	0.20	(0.05	0.21	(0.07)
* Commuting d. of spouse [d]	0.13	(0.05)	0.15	(0.05)	0.06	(0.05)
* Wage rate [c]	-1.27	(0.66)	-1.63	(0.54)	-1.71	(0.58)
* Male	0.56	(0.39)	0.65	(0.37)	0.40	(0.32)
* Civil servant	0.22	(0.36)	-0.13	(0.28)	0.23	(0.21)
* > 32 hours	-0.87	(0.47)	-0.62	(0.33)	-0.99	(0.40)
* University	1.06	(0.88)	0.66	(0.52)	0.84	(0.53)
* Owner	0.14	(0.32)	0.13	(0.28)	0.23	(0.21)
* Wage/spouse's w.	0.01	(0.02)	0.01	(0.02)	0.01	(0.02)
* Masspoints and probabilities						
u_1	-1.42	(2.06)	-0.51	(1.92)	1.72	(1.72)

Table 9.1 continued

$u_2 - u_1$			-2.27	(0.88)	-2.28	(0.46)
P_1	1.00[(e)]		0.99	(0.01)		
P_2			0.01	(0.01)		
P_{11}					0.98	(0.01)
$P_{21} = P_{12}$					0.01	(0.00)
P_{22}					0.00[(e)]	
* Correlation					0.01	(0.08)
Loglikelihood	120.24		114.22		110.08	

(a) Standard errors in parentheses.
(b) Reference groups: type age (older than 44), size of branch (less than 20), number of subordinates (more than 3).
(c) Logarithm of net wage per hour (in Dutch guilders).
(d) Distance in 10 kilometres, one-way.
(e) Coefficient is fixed as explained in the text.

The Specification Revisited

The results presented above rely on a range of assumptions, which we will critically reconsider in this section. First, we have in our analysis originally assumed a time-stationary hazard rate, implying an exponential distribution for the job durations. As an alternative, we have decided to considered also a non-stationary hazard rate, by assuming a Weibull distribution. This implies that the hazard rate $\theta(t_i|v_i,x)$ can be written as $\alpha t_i^{\alpha-1} v_i.\exp(x.\beta_i)$, i =1, 2. Note that when $\alpha = 1.00$, the Weibull distribution is identical to the exponential distribution. Estimation of the model assuming a Weibull distribution showed next that α equals 0.92 with a standard error of 0.17. Hence, the hypothesis that $\alpha = 1.00$ is not refuted. So, we do not reject the assumption that job mobility is not duration dependent.

Second, we have initially assumed that the mixing distribution can be described by means of two masspoints. Including a third masspoint shows that the third masspoint takes on the same value as one of the other two masspoints. Hence, the assumption on the discrete mixing distribution seems valid.

Third, our initial estimation procedure had assumed that the bivariate mixing distribution is symmetric, so assuming that $v_{11} = v_{12}$, $v_{21} = v_{22}$ and $\gamma_1 = \gamma_2$. We have re-estimated therefore the model relaxing this assumption and tested the restrictions using a standard Likelihood Ratio test. We found that the restrictions are valid at a 5% significance level and that the point estimates hardly change. In particular, the difference between the value of the masspoints are almost identical for males and females (v_{11}-v_{12} = -2.23; v_{21}-v_{22} = -2.19).

Fourth, we have re-estimated the model while changing the set of the explanatory variables. We have used the wage of the spouse instead of the ratio of the wage over the spouse's wage. Again, we found no effect. In addition, we have added a variable which measures the distance between the workplaces of worker and the spouse's workplace. The expected effect of the latter variable is positive according to search theory, however, we failed to show an effect of this particular variable.

Conclusion

In many studies on duration of stay of individuals, it has been found that unobserved variables play a crucial role. The study of joint duration distributions in which the dependence is induced through mixing has resulted in few theoretical and empirical results in the literature. In the current chapter, we have analysed stock sampled durations observations. We have investigated the consequences of the inclusion of unobserved variables that affect a worker's job mobility jointly with the unobserved variables that affect the job mobility of the worker's spouse. This is done by the use of a bivariate mixing distribution.

We find that the differences in the outcomes of a model ignoring heterogeneity and a model employing a univariate or bivariate mixing distribution are not substantial. However, although the estimated effects of the explanatory variables on job mobility are not strongly affected by allowing for mutual dependence between the unobserved variables, the effects of the explanatory variables have been estimated more precisely by allowing for this dependence.

PART IV

EMPIRICAL APPLICATIONS OF COMMUTING AND ON-THE-JOB SEARCH BEHAVIOUR

10.   The Determinants of Commuting Distance

Introduction

In this chapter we investigate the effect of residential and job moving behaviour on commuting distance. The data set used here (called Telepanel), collected in 1992-1993, includes the complete life course pattern of Dutch respondents, including the labour, residential and family career. The data were collected in a retrospective way. We select those persons who were employed in January 1985, and observe commuting behaviour until December 1991. Moreover, those who became employed between January 1985 and December 1991 were also included in the analysis. From this data set, we selected those who are employed for more than 32 hours per week and for which all relevant data are observed. This provides us with observations on the commuting behaviour of 548 persons. Note that for a large number of persons we have multiple observations on commuting behaviour (those who change job or residence during the period of observation). In our data set 26% of the persons change their commuting distance by more than 5 kilometres. Furthermore, for a large number of observations, we observe that their characteristics change over time; this may or may not affect their commuting behaviour (48% of the persons who live with their parents at the beginning of the period under observation leave their parental house during the period under observation). To employ all this statistical information, we measure commuting distance every year (in January). This enables us to include information on multiple observations. In total, we have 3011 yearly observations. So, on average, we observe more than five observations (3011/548) on each individual. As this is a longitudinal data set, we observe the choices of the individuals over time. This provides a means of increasing the efficiency of the estimates, and improves interpretation of the coefficients.[1]

Empirical Model

Precise information about commuting distance or commuting time is missing in the data set, as only information on the municipality of residence and workplace of the worker is available. So commuting distance y_{it} (i= 1,...,548; t = 1985,..,1991) is measured as (the logarithm of) the distance between the centres of the respective municipalities. For those who work in the same municipality as where they live, we assume that commuting distance is less than a certain level r. In the empirical application we have safely assumed that r equals 5 kilometres.[2] We assume a linear specification in the explanatory variables x_{it}:

$$y_{it} = \beta\, x_{it} + \eta_i + u_{it}$$

where u_{it} is the error term and η_i the individual-specific error term. Consistent, though inefficient estimates for the coefficients β can be obtained by ignoring the correlations among the errors and using a Tobit estimation method for the pooled data (Maddala, 1985).[3] For this case, the loglikelihood of commuting distance can be written as:

$$LogL = \sum_{i=1}^{3011} (1 - \mathrm{dum}_{it})$$

where $\mathrm{dum}_{it} = 1$ when commuting distance is observed, and $\mathrm{dum}_{it} = 0$ otherwise; f is the normal density with mean zero and variance σ^2_u, and F is the normal distribution which corresponds to f. However, more efficient estimates for the determinants of commuting distance can be obtained by use of the fact that we have a panel of repeated observations. One possibility is to make normality assumptions about the distribution of η, a so-called random effect model. The loglikelihood of commuting distance can then be written as:

$$LogL = \sum_{i=1}^{548} \log \int \prod_{t=1985}^{1991} [F(r - \beta' x_{it} - \eta)]^{1-\mathrm{dum}_{it}} f(y_{it} - \beta' x_{it} - \eta)^{\mathrm{dum}_{it}} dN(\eta)$$

Where N is a normal cumulative distribution with mean zero and variance σ^2_n. We will report estimates of the pooled data and the data while imposing a panel structure.

We include those (time-varying) explanatory variables which are expected to affect commuting distance. We distinguish among individuals who live with their parents, with their spouse (employed or nonemployed), with or without children, or alone. Moreover, we include dummies for gender, age groups and educational achievement. We also include a trend variable to allow for the effect that commuting distances increase over time in the Netherlands.[4] It is important to notice that many potentially interesting variables are excluded from the analysis as these are endogenous with respect to commuting (e.g. the wage rate).

In chapter 5 we have analysed the consequence of market imperfections on commuting behaviour from a theoretical point of view. Market imperfections are thought to prevent households from adjusting the commuting distance to the optimal level. So the probability of moving job and the probability of moving residence are expected to affect commuting. These variables are however endogenous with respect to commuting behaviour, because individuals are more likely to move when commuting costs are high. One way to overcome this statistical difficulty is to include the *predicted* value of the probability to move job[5] and the *predicted* value of the probability to move residence[6] as regressors.[7] It should be noted that in some empirical investigations of commuting behaviour, information on mobility in the past has been used to explain the influence of market imperfections on commuting distance (White, 1986; Madden, 1981; Singell and Lillydahl, 1986; Dubin, 1991[8]). We include dummies for workers who have moved job or residence last year (the endogeneity of these variables is acknowledged).

Empirical Results

We estimate the panel model by ML using Gaussian quadrature (Butler and Moffit (1982).[9] The estimates can be found in Table 10.1. Notice that the individual specific variance σ_n is much larger than the variance σ_u. The relatively large value for the individual-specific variance σ_n causes a correlation of about 0.80 between the sequential disturbances (of course, this is due to the fact that in about 80% of the cases, workers neither change residence nor job in a certain year). The very high correlation between the disturbances makes clear that pooling the data is less efficient and thus explains the higher standard errors for the estimates of the pooled data (Table 10.1). Notice that pooling the data or using a panel model renders different estimates for the coefficients of the variables educational achievement, parents, children. We will discuss now the outcome of the estimates for the panel model, as these are likely to be more precise.

Table 10.1   Empirical Estimates of Coefficients for Commuting Distance

standard errors in parentheses; * = significant at 5%.

Variables	panel structure		pooled	
*constant	0.71	(0.17)*	-0.50	(0.29)
*male	0.21	(0.04)*	0.36	(0.07)*
*age groups				
< age < 24	0.46	(0.08)*	0.73	(0.20)*
24 < age < 34	0.41	(0.08)*	0.57	(0.15)*
34 < age < 44	0.23	(0.06)*	0.13	(0.11)
*educational level				
university/ polytechnic	0.03	(0.05)	0.35	(0.08)*
vocational	-0.18	(0.04)	-0.32	(0.08)*
*household situation				
with spouse	0.18	(0.05)*	0.59	(0.11)*
with parents	0.05	(0.05)	0.66	(0.12)*
*working status spouse				
employed	0.79	(0.05)*	0.43	(0.08)*
*children	0.10	(0.04)*	0.03	(0.07)
*trend variable	0.04	(0.01)*	0.06	(0.02)*
σ_η^2(individual-specific)	0.99	(0.02)*		
loglikelihood	-4039.13		-4101.61	

Workers are expected to exhibit different commuting patterns if they differ in their positions in the housing or labour market. Young workers who just entered the labour market with lower wages and place utility are more likely to accept non-compensated commuting costs because they know that these costs are temporary. Moreover, older workers are more likely to have found a job with lower commuting costs in the past.[10] In line with these expectations, the panel model results indicate that commuting decreases with age. Similar findings for the Netherlands are reported by, among others, Rouwendal and Rietveld (1994) and Camstra (1995).[11]

Surprisingly, and in contrast to Rouwendal and Rietveld (1994), we find that educational achievement has no affect on commuting.[12] In line with the literature, we observe that the household situation affects commuting behaviour. Those who live with a spouse or have children apparently commute more. The results show that those with a working spouse commute significantly more. This is possibly related to a poor ability to adapt their housing situation to their work location. Our finding that women commute less is in line with most other empirical findings (Madden, 1981). In line with studies on aggregate data, we find that commuting distance has increased during the period under observation (at a rate of 4% each year, according to this study).[13]

Recall that the theoretical search model indicates that individuals who are more likely to move residence or job (e.g. due to lower moving costs) reach preferred positions at lower costs, and will therefore reach a more favourable situation as time passes. This may explain our empirical result that those who are more likely to move job have smaller commuting distances.[14] But we do not find any effect for the predicted probability to move residence. These results seem to support the findings of Dubin (1991), Siegel (1975) and Simpson (1980), see Chapter 2, that the employment location is more responsive to the residential location than the residential location is to the job location (due to high residential moving costs).

We also find that workers commute more if they have moved job last year, while residential moving behaviour has no effect.[15] The result that workers commute more if they have moved job recently may be due to different factors. It may be that longer commuting distances are *temporarily* accepted. Alternatively, it might be that as the costs of commuting are decreasing over time, workers accept jobs which are, on average, further from the home location. Rouwendal and Rietveld (1994) also conclude that the apparently rapid increase in commuting distance during the period considered is due in large part to changes in the employment situation, while residential moves are more or less neutral in their effect on the average commuting distance.

Despite the fact that many variables are statistically significant in the analysis, we find that the predictive power of the estimated models is low. The implied correlation between the predicted commuting distance and the observed commuting distance is about 0.03. The failure to explain observed differences in commuting distance is universally found.[16] One explanation might be that virtually all influential explanatory variables are missing in the statistical model. A more satisfying interpretation, which corresponds to the assumptions of the search model, is that workers do not choose a residence-job combination that offers a unique optimal commuting distance, but they do accept *a wide range* of combinations of jobs and residences while they search for better jobs and residences. In flexible labour markets, it will not be worthwhile for the worker to adjust the residential location, and, as a result, workers become footloose (Hamilton, 1982, 1989). Policies which aim to reduce commuting will therefore hardly be effective in the short run, especially if they are not accompanied by measures which reduce the costs of moving residence.

Conclusion

The empirical results support the hypothesis that commuting distance is negatively related to the probability of moving job. Those workers who are more mobile in the labour market will attain a more favourable situation as time passes. This supports the hypothesis that workers search in the labour market for better commuting alternatives. It is noted that a similar effect of the probability of moving residence on commuting has not been identified. This may support earlier findings that the employment location is more responsive to the residential location than the residential location is to the job location.

The policy implications are based on the notion that workers search for better jobs and residences. Workers do not choose a residence-job combination which offers a unique optimal commuting distance, but accept *a wide range* of combinations of jobs and residences as they search for better jobs and residences. Policies which aim at reducing commuting - e.g. policies which reduce the costs of moving residence or moving job - will therefore hardly be effective in the short run. In the long run however, positive effects of these policies are expected as workers may obtain shorter commuting distances at lesser costs.

Notes

[1] For example, given the pooled data, we find that two-earner households commute 43% more than single wage-earners. This result may be interpreted that all two-earner households commute 43% more (so two-earner households are homogeneous), or that 50% of the two-earner households commute 86% more, and the other 50% has the same commute as single wage-earners. In the case of panel data, we find that two-earner households commute 79% more than single wage-earners.

[2] A sensitivity analysis showed that the results are scarcely affected by an increase or decrease of a few kilometres.

[3] The existence of individual-specific effects implies a correlation between the disturbances of commuting distance at different time periods for the same individual. This correlation equals $\sigma^2_n/(\sigma^2_n + \sigma^2_u)$.

[4] We tested the assumption of a linear increase in commuting distance by replacing the trend variable by calendar dummies. The results indicated that the use of a trend variable is not restrictive.

[5] The probability to move job has been estimated for the pooled data conditional on a large number of regressors. We include dummies for gender, age groups (age < 24, 24 < age < 34, 34 < age < 44), size of branch (size > 200, 20 < size < 200), number of subordinates (number = 0, 0 < number < 4), ln(wage rate), educational level (university/polytechnic, vocational), calendar year dummies (85/86,87/88,89/90), spouse employed, employed in private sector. The empirical results can be found in Appendix 10.1.

[6] The probability to move residence has been estimated for the pooled data conditional on: age groups (age < 24, 24 < age < 34, 34 < age < 44), complete house, children, with spouse, with parents, owner, educational level (university/polytechnic, vocational), calendar year dummies (85/86,87/88,89/90). The results can be found in Appendix 10.1.

[7] The estimates of the standard errors are not under-estimated given this procedure. In Appendix 10.2, we present the results of the same model, excluding the predicted values for job and residential mobility. These results show that the standard errors of the regressors are in the same order of magnitude whether the predicted values are included or not.

[8] In these studies, the following effects are reported. White (1986) finds that residence tenure has a significant negative effect on commuting. Madden (1981) finds a negative effect for job tenure. Singell and Lillydahl (1986) find that in two-earner households that recently changed their residence, male commute times decline while female commute times increase, although this effect may reverse when females' earnings exceed males'. Dubin (1991) reports that residential mobility has relatively little importance on the extent to which workers use firm decentralisation to shorten their commutes, but job mobility is important.

[9] This procedure avoids numerical integration by approximating the normal distribution N by a discrete number of points. It turned out that eight points were needed to approximate N sufficiently.

[10] This argument is analogous to Burdett (1978), who points out that wages rise with years of work experience, because workers with greater experience are more likely to have found a higher paying job.

[11] In both papers however, the authors propose a different explanation (namely cohort effects).

[12] Educational achievement is however significant when the data are pooled.

[13] It is noted that if the measures for residential and job mobility are excluded (Appendix 11.2), then the estimate for the trend variable equals 2%. This may have a simple explanation. Those who are observed over a considerable period of time (in our data set 7 years) are expected to decrease their commuting distance in a stationary environment as they search for better job-residence combinations. As a result, those who are more likely to move will have shorter distances to travel. In a non-stationary environment, this will cause the estimate for the trend variable to be downward biased.

[14] The inclusion of the 4 mobility variables increases the loglikelihood from -4064.85 to -4039.13, so the effect of these variables are significant at the 1% significant level.

[15] A similar analysis with elapsed job and residence durations leads to the same conclusion (i.e. the elapsed job duration has a significant negative effect on commuting; the elapsed residence duration does not have a significant effect on commuting).

[16] See, for example, White (1986).

Appendix 10.1

Table 10.2   Empirical estimates of coefficients for voluntary job-to-job and residential mobility (probit model on pooled data)

standard errors in paratheses; *: significant at 5%.

variables	residential mobility		job mobility	
* constant	-1.04	(0.23) *	0.22	(0.34) *
* males				
* *age*				
< age < 24	0.83	(0.15) *	0.91	(0.14) *
24 < age < 34	0.80	(0.14) *	0.57	(0.12)*
34 < age < 44	0.50	(0.13) *	0.42	(0.12) *
size of branch				
size > 200 p	-0.26	(0.08)		
20 p < size < 200 p	-0.23	(0.08)		
* *number of subordinates*				
0	-0.17	(0.09)		
1,2,3	0.06	(0.10)		
* private sector	0.15	(0.07) *		
* ln(wage/hour)	-0.63	(0.10) *		
* 'complete house'	-0.56	(0.16) *		
* less than 4 rooms	0.42	(0.12) *		
* children	-0.07	(0.10)		

Table 10.2 Continued

* household situation				
with spouse	-0.21	(0.10)		
with parents	-0.36	(0.16)		
* earning couple	0.12	(0.08)	0.03	(0.08)
* owner	-0.43	(0.08) *		
* educational level				
university/polytechnic	0.03	(0.10)	0.30	(0.12) *
vocational	-0.14	(0.09)	-0.19	(0.10)
* calendar year				
1985/1986	0.15	(0.11)	-0.37	(0.10) *
1987/1988	0.25	(0.11) *	-0.13	(0.10)
1989/1990	0.14	(0.11)	-0.07	(0.10)
Loglikelihood	-690.17		-1000.94	

Appendix 10.2

Table 10.3 Empirical estimates of coefficients for commuting distance
standard errors in paratheses; *: significant at 5%.

variables

	panel structure		pooled	
* constant	1.12	(0.07)*	1.06	(0.14) *
* male	0.35	(0.04)*	0.34	(0.07) *
* age groups				
< age < 24	0.24	(0.06)*	-0.10	(0.13)
24 < age < 34	0.29	(0.04)*	0.00	(0.09)
34 < age < 44	0.08	(0.04)	-0.23	(0.09) *
* educational level				
university/ polytechnic	0.00	(0.05)	0.26	(0.08) *
vocational	0.05	(0.04)	-0.19	(0.07) *
* household situation				
with spouse	0.23	(0.05) *	0.67	(0.10) *
with parents	0.14	(0.06) *	0.60	(0.12) *
* working status spouse				
employed	0.38	(0.04) *	0.33	(0.07) *
* children	0.17	(0.04) *	0.07	(0.07)
* trend variable	0.02	(0.01) *	0.02	(0.01) *
σ_u^2	0.47	(0.01) *	1.46	(0.05) *
σ_η^2 (individual-specific)	0.93	(0.02) *		
loglikelihood	-4064.85	-4119.35		

11. On-The-Job Search: The Importance of Commuting Time

Introduction

In recent years, policy makers and researchers have become increasingly interested in the question of how individuals react to increases in travel costs and travel time due to congestion or road pricing (Banister, 1993; Rietveld, 1993; Verhoef, 1994). Given increases in the monetary or time costs of road usage, it is thought that car users may switch to other modes, may change departure time or may forego route trips (Emmerink, Nijkamp and Rietveld, 1996). In particular, research has focused on commuters who travel mostly during peak hours (Arnott, de Palma and Lindsey, 1990,1994).

As an alternative, commuters may change job or residence in order to decrease commuting costs. As far as we know, this issue has not received any attention in the transport economics literature, although it has received considerable attention in the labour and housing market literature (Zax, 1991a). In the labour market literature, it is common to analyse job moving behaviour by using job search models. The basic point of departure is that workers receive job offers, which arrive randomly. Workers have to decide whether to accept or refuse the wage offered by an employer. Many variations of this model exist (Mortensen, 1986 for a review). For example, one may extend the model by the introduction of search effort (Albrecht, Holmlund and Lang, 1991). Hence, job offers do not arrive at random, but they arrive as a result of a search effort decision. Furthermore, one may extend the model by including commuting and residential moving behaviour (see chapter 3) or by assuming that workers belong to a two-earner household (see chapter 4). In this chapter, the theoretical considerations will be based on search theory.

It has been noticed before that a striking characteristic of search theory is the ability to generate rather precise predictions (Devine and Kiefer, 1993). Many of these predictions are, in principle, empirically testable. Tests will certainly increase - or decrease - the credibility of the theoretical search model proposed. The search model analysed in the current chapter makes rather precise predictions about workers' job search effort as a function of commuting time. Job search effort is *increasing* in commuting time - whatever the behaviour in the housing market - and, under some conditions, *convex* in commuting time. The latter result implies that if the commuting time increases from 45 to 60 minutes, the response will be much stronger than if the commuting time increases from 30 to 45 minutes. We will show that the latter result may hold, because the probability of accepting a job offer is increasing with commuting time *and* the lifetime utility associated with the current job is decreasing with commuting time. The search model may make this prediction even if we specify the commuting costs (the disutility of commuting) as a linear function of commuting time. Furthermore, we demonstrate that workers are not likely to be not very responsive to commuting costs due to future job and residential moves. Consequently, we show theoretically that it may be rational for workers to be non responsive to increases in commuting time given shorter commuting times, and to be responsive to increases in commuting time given longer commuting times. In the empirical part of the chapter, we provide some support for this theoretical result based on a data set of Dutch commuters.

This result may have some important implications for research on commuting behaviour. A common assumption in the economic literature is that workers choose their residence and job locations optimally such that the commuting costs are compensated in the labour market (by higher wages) and housing market (by lower housing prices). Recent empirical results, based on aggregated data, indicate, however, that commuters are rather 'footloose' and are more willing to commute than predicted by static urban models (Hamilton, 1982, 1989). This implies that workers are not responsive to small, or even substantial deviations from the 'long-run' optimal commuting time (Crane, 1996). In the current chapter, we are able to establish a similar result, theoretically, based on sound micro economic principles without imposing an urban model, and, empirically, based on micro data on job search behaviour.

Search Theory

Introduction

Our objective is to derive a framework that explains the job search behaviour of employed individuals who explicitly take into account commuting costs and residential moving behaviour. The relationship between job search behaviour and commuting will be described from a search-theoretical perspective. Search theory is appealing as it is based on the idea that individuals maximise lifetime utility by moving through different states and so it is explicitly dynamic. We assume that job and residence offers arrive as a result of search effort. So, job and residential moving behaviour is due to a combination of chance - the arrival of an offer - and a decision-making process - the decision to search with a certain effort and the decision to accept an offer.

Since the seminal papers of Stigler (1961, 1962), job search theory has become one of the main theoretical and empirical tools for understanding the working of the labour market. Recently, Devine and Kiefer (1993) argue that more attention should be paid to nonwage characteristics.

In principle, search theory can readily be applied to determine the optimal search intensity in the labour and housing market. Workers are thought of as facing a set of alternative dwellings and a set of alternative employment alternatives. Every combination of dwelling and job location uniquely determines the commuting distance. Conditional on the commuting distance, the worker chooses the mode of transport that determines the commuting time. Hence, we focus mainly on the relationship between the optimal choice of job search intensity and commuting time.

The Model

The point of departure is that individuals are employed and search for better jobs and dwellings. Individuals derive utility from the wage w, place utility r and commuting time z. Place utility is defined as the utility experienced in a location, net of housing costs. Notice that the effect of commuting *time* is assumed. Alternatively, one may assume that commuting *distance* or a combination of time and distance affects instantaneous utility. Thus, the instantaneous utility v experienced in a certain period of length Δt is a function of w, r and z and is equal to $v(w,r,z) \Delta t$.

We assume that $\partial v/\partial w > 0$, $\partial v/\partial z < 0$ and $\partial v/\partial r > 0$. Hence, instantaneous utility increases with wage and place utility, and decreases with commuting time. We assume that v is concave in w, r and z. The once-only loss in instantaneous utility due to moving job or moving residence equal c_1 and c_2, respectively.

The person searches in the labour market with intensity s_1 at a cost of $k_1(s_1)$. Search costs are increasing and convex in s_1 ($k_1'(s_1) = 0$ and $k_1''(s_1) = 0$). Jobs arrive with arrival rate $p_1(s_1)$ The job arrival rate p_1 is increasing and concave in s_1 ($p_1'(s_1) = 0$ and $p_1''(s_1) = 0$). Similarly, the residential search costs $k_2(s_2)$ are increasing and convex in s_2 ($k_2(s_2)' = 0$ and $k_2(s_2)'' = 0$. Dwellings arrive with arrival rate p_2. The residence arrival rates are increasing and concave in s_2. Moreover, we suppose that the effects of the search costs k_1 and k_2 on the instantaneous utility function are additive. Pooling of offers is not allowed: job and dwelling offers have to be refused or accepted before other offers arrive.

A job offer is entirely characterised by the wage offer, w_x, and the commuting time offer, z_x. Wage and commuting time offers are random drawings from a bivariate distribution F_{wz}. Similarly, a dwelling offer is entirely characterised by the place utility offer, r_x, and commuting time offer, z_x. Place utility and commuting time offers are random drawings from a distribution F_{rz}. The wage is received until a new job is accepted; similarly, the place utility is experienced until the individual changes residence. The commuting time is borne until the individuals leaves either the job or the residence. We suppose that w, r and z obtain non-negative values. Finally, we assume that the structural parameters of the model (c_i, $p_i(s_i)$, $k_i(s_i)$, i=1,2; v, F_{wz} and F_{rz}) are stationary over time and over space.

The expected lifetime utility received from the current wage, place utility and commuting time is denoted by V(w,r,z). V includes the possibility of offers in the future. Benefits and costs are discounted at rate ρ. The individual is assumed to maximise lifetime utility V. The individual has to decide whether to accept a job or residence offer, taking into account the expected offers in the future. A job offer will be accepted if $V(w_x,r,z_x) - c_1 - V(w,r,z) > 0$, otherwise the offer will be rejected. Consequently, given a job offer, a worker will obtain the maximum of $[V(w_x,r,z_x) - c_1, V(w,r,z)]$. Similarly, a residence offer will be accepted if $V(w,r_x,z_x) - c_2 - V(w,r,z) > 0$. So, given a residence offer, a worker will obtain the maximum of $[V(w,r_x,z_x) - c_2, V(w,r,z)]$.

Consider an interval Δt. The lifetime utility for an employed person is then (Mortensen 1986, Albrecht, Holmlund and Lang 1991):

$$V(w,r,z) = \frac{1}{1+\rho\Delta t}\{v(w,r,z)\Delta t - k_1(s_1)\Delta t - k_2(s_2)\Delta t$$
$$+ p_1(s_1)\Delta t E \max[V(w_x,r,z_x) - c_1, V(w,r,z)]$$
$$+ p_2(s_2)\Delta t E \max[V(w,r_x,z_x) - c_2, V(w,r,z)]$$
$$+ (1 - (p_1(s_1) + p_2(s_2))\Delta t)V(w,r,z) + o(\Delta t)\}.$$

In this equation, the expectation is taken with respect to the variables which have a subscript 'x'. So, given a job offer, the expectation is taken with respect to the distribution of the wage and commuting time; given a residence offer, the expectation is taken with respect to the distribution of the place utility and commuting time. The interpretation of this equation is straightforward. The instantaneous utility minus the search costs is proportional to the length Δt of the time interval. With probability $p_1\Delta t$ a job offer will be received and the worker will obtain the expected maximum of $[V(w_x,r,z_x) - c_1, V(w,r,z)]$. With probability $p_2\Delta t$ a residence offer will be received and the worker will obtain the expected maximum of $[V(w,r_x,z_x) - c_2, V(w,r,z)]$. With probability $1 - (p_1 + p_2)\Delta t$, the worker will receive neither a job nor a residence offer. The last term reflects the notion that as Δt approaches zero any non proportionality of utility to the length of the time interval goes to zero at an even faster rate (Albrecht, Holmlund and Lang, 1991).

One may prove that the probability of receiving a job and a residence offer simultaneously goes to zero if the length of the time interval goes to zero. Hence, the model excludes the possibility that residence and job offers *arrive* simultaneously, although the models allows workers to *search* simultaneously for jobs and residences (s_1 and s_2 are both positive).

From now on, we will treat the worker's decision problem in continuous time to simplify the analysis. Thus, we rewrite V, dividing by Δt, and let Δt approach zero. This gives:

$$\rho V(w,r,z) = v(w,r,z) - k_1(s_1) - k_2(s_2)$$
$$+ p_1(s_1)E \max[V(w_x,r,z_x) - c_1 - V(w,r,z), 0]$$
$$+ p_2(s_2)E \max[V(w,r_x,z_x) - c_2 - V(w,r,z), 0].$$

Hence, lifetime utility can be written as the sum of the instantaneous utility and the expected benefit of accepting a residential or job offer, discounted at rate ρ. The worker experiences currently instantaneous utility minus search costs. At rate p_1 (p_2) a job (residence) offer will be received, and that offer will be accepted if the value of the new position exceeds that of the current position plus the moving costs. Bellman's principle ensures that the above formula defines the value of V and the optimal acceptance rules (Mortensen, 1986; Albrecht, Holmlund and Lang, 1991). It is then straightforward to show that lifetime utility V is increasing in w and r, and decreasing in z, c_1 and c_2.

According to the search model, job and residential moving behaviour are described by transition rates. We denote the transition rate of moving from the current job to another job as θ_w, which can be written as the product of the job arrival rate p_1 and the probability of accepting a job offer P_w. So, P_w is defined as $\int_A dF_{wz}$ where $A = \{V(w_x,r,z_x)-c_1>V(w,r,z)\}$. Hence, $\theta_w = p_1 \cdot P_w$. Similarly, the transition rate of moving residence is denoted as θ_r, which can be written as the product of the residential arrival rate p_2 and the probability of accepting a residence offer P_r. So, $\theta_r = p_2 \cdot P_r$, where $P_r = \int_B dF_{wz}$ where $B = \{V(w,r_x,z_x)-c_2>V(w,r,z)\}$. It has been shown that $\partial P_w/\partial z = 0$ and $\partial P_r/\partial z = 0$. Hence, the probability of accepting a job or residence offer is non-decreasing in z. Moreover, it appears that $\partial P_w/\partial c_1 = 0$ and $\partial P_r/\partial c_2 = 0$. The probability of accepting a job (residence) offer is non-increasing in the job (residential) moving costs.

The Optimal Search Strategy

In this section, the theoretical comparative effects of z on search effort in the labour market are examined (the effects on search effort in the housing market can be derived similarly). The optimal choice of search effort s_1 is derived using the first-order condition $\partial V(w,r,z)/\partial s_1 = 0$. The optimal choice of s_1 can be obtained by differentiating the last equation with respect to s_1, and setting the resultant to zero:

$$\frac{\partial k_1}{\partial s_1} + \frac{\partial p_1}{\partial s_1} E \max[V(w_x,r,z_x) - c_1 - V(w,r,z),0] = 0.$$

The interpretation of this equation is straightforward. The marginal cost of search effort equals the marginal expected benefit of search. We denote the expected benefit of search as Emax. The marginal expected benefit of search can be written as the marginal job arrival rate times the expected benefit of receiving a job offer. The second-order condition is that the left-hand side is decreasing in s_i. The concavity of p_i and the convexity of k_i in their arguments ensure that this condition will be satisfied. In the case that there is no solution for $s_i > 0$, then $s_i = 0$. We will limit our analysis to the interesting case that $s_i > 0$, which requires that $P_w > 0$ (when $P_w = 0$, all job offers will be rejected, so there is no incentive to search in the labour market).

Search Effort as a Function of Commuting Time

The comparative statics effects of z on s_i can be readily derived by differentiating the first-order condition. It can be shown that the sign of $\partial s_i / \partial z$ equals the sign of $\partial E\max/\partial z$, where

$$\frac{\partial E\max}{\partial z} = -\frac{\partial V(w, r, z)}{\partial z} P_w.$$

Hence, $\partial E\max/\partial z > 0$, because $\partial V/\partial z < 0$. As a result, $\partial s_i/\partial z > 0$. Hence, search effort is increasing in commuting time, since the expected benefit of accepting a job offer is increasing in commuting time. The expected benefit is increasing in commuting time, since the lifetime utility associated with the current job is decreasing in commuting time. Surprisingly perhaps, this result does *not* need any restrictive assumption on housing market behaviour. For example, this result also holds when search effort in the housing market is strongly increasing in commuting time. We will demonstrate now that uncertainty about future job and residential locations - so θ_w or θ_r is large - prevents commuters from reacting strongly to the commuting time, so $\partial s_i/\partial z$ will be small. It can be shown that

$$\frac{\partial V}{\partial z} = \frac{v'(z)}{\rho + \theta_w + \theta_r}.$$

This equation has a straightforward interpretation: the marginal change in *lifetime* utility equals the marginal change in *instantaneous* utility discounted by the sum of the discount rate and the job mobility and residential mobility rates. One can infer now that the larger are θ_w and θ_r, the less negative is $\partial V/\partial z$ (recall that $\partial v/\partial z$ is negative). As a consequence, the larger are θ_w and θ_r, the smaller is $\partial E\max/\partial z$. This implies that $\partial s_i/\partial z$ will be small when θ_w or θ_r are large. Hence, search effort levels do not respond strongly to the costs induced by the journey between work and home due to uncertainty caused by future job and residential moving behaviour.

A question we would like to answer is whether $\partial s_1/\partial z$ is increasing, or decreasing in z - so we will examine the sign of $\partial^2 s_1/(\partial z)^2$. To answer this question, additional assumptions on $p_1(s)$ and $k_1(s)$ are needed. We will assume that $p_1'''(s_1) = 0$ and $k_1'''(s_1) = 0$. It can be shown that $\partial s_1/\partial z$ is increasing in z, if the following condition hold:

$$\frac{\partial^2 V}{(\partial z)^2} P_w + \frac{\partial V}{\partial z}\frac{\partial P_w}{\partial z} \leq 0.$$

To understand this condition, recall that lifetime utility is decreasing in commuting time and the probability of accepting a job offer is increasing in commuting time. Hence, the second term on the left side is negative, which implies that $\partial s_1/\partial z$ is increasing in z. In consequence, search effort may be a convex function of commuting time, because the probability of accepting a job offer is increasing in commuting time *and* the lifetime utility associated with the current job is decreasing in commuting time. In contrast to the second term, the sign of the first term is ambiguous. It can be shown that the sign of $\partial^2 V/(\partial z)^2$ is not determined. To explain why the sign of $\partial^2 V/(\partial z)^2$ is not determined, we will focus on two extreme cases (case A and case B).

Case A. Suppose that the job and residential mobility rates are zero. This implies that $\partial^2 V/(\partial z)^2$ equals $\partial^2 v/(\partial z)^2/\partial$. So, the second derivative of lifetime utility is determined by the second derivative of the instantaneous utility function v, which is *assumed* to be nonpositive (v is concave in its arguments). It is worthwhile emphasising the fact that the latter assumption is the only assumption that fits within standard consumption theory. If commuting time increases, leisure time - which is a consumption good - decreases. The law of diminishing marginal utility of consumption guarantees then that v is concave in commuting time. As a consequence, the condition holds.

Case B. Suppose that $\partial^2 v/(\partial z)^2$ is zero, whereas the job and residential mobility rates are positive. Given this assumption, the current level of commuting time will change due to a job or residence move. The longer the commuting time, the greater the probability that the current level of commuting time will be reduced in the future. As a result, it can be shown that $\partial^2 V/(\partial z)^2$ is positive. As a consequence, the condition may not always hold. For example, it can be shown that if $\partial^2 v/(\partial z)^2 = \theta_r = \rho = 0$, then the condition does not hold.

In consequence, we have shown that the sign of $\partial^2 s/(\partial z)^2$ is ambiguous. When the job and residential mobility rates are not strongly responsive to commuting time, the sign of $\partial^2 s/(\partial z)^2$ is positive. The latter case seems to be the most common situation. Hence, in general, job search effort is convex in commuting time.

Notice that search effort may be convex in commuting time even if the instantaneous utility function v is linear in commuting time ($\partial^2 v/(\partial z)^2 = 0$). Consequently, an empirical finding that job search effort is convex in commuting time does *not* imply that the disutility of commuting is convex in commuting time. Moreover, the condition that residential mobility is absent ($\theta_r = 0$) is not a sufficient condition to guarantee that $\partial^2 s_1/(\partial z)^2$ is positive.

Our results are based on the notion that $\partial P_w/\partial z > 0$, i.e. the probability of accepting a job is increasing in commuting time. Interestingly, others have also noted before that the probability of accepting a job offer is a convex function of commuting time given a fixed residential location (Seater, 1979; Rouwendal and Rietveld, 1994). This would imply that $\partial^2 P_w/(\partial z)^2 > 0$. Let us explain this result by means of an example. Given the absence of heterogeneity of wages (i.e. all wages offered equal the current wage), given the absence of job moving costs and given a fixed residential location, the search model predicts that probability of accepting a job is proportional to the *square* of commuting time. Only jobs at a commuting time that is less than the current commuting time are accepted. The probability of receiving a commuting time offer that is less than the current commuting time z is proportional to πz^2 as the acceptance region is a circle. Hence $P_w = c.z^2$, $c > 0$ and thus $\partial^2 P_w/(\partial z)^2 = 2.c > 0$. A priority, it may seem that if $\partial^2 P_w/(\partial z)^2 > 0$, then $\partial^3 s_1/(\partial z)^3 > 0$. One may show however that this is not necessarily the case. In the case that $\partial^2 V/(\partial z)^2$ is negative, then $\partial^3 s_1/(\partial z)^3 > 0$ (this can be shown by differentiating $\partial^2 Emax/(\partial z)^2$ with respect to z). This implies that search effort levels are low given low commuting times, and rise sharply at a certain level z.

The Effect of Residential Moving Costs c_2

Households differ strongly in residential mobility behaviour due to differences in residential moving costs and the household characteristics. For example, single wage earners may more easily move residence to reduce commuting time than workers who belong to a two-earner household. Differences in residential moving behaviour are captured in the above model by the residential moving costs c_2 and the residence arrival rate p_2. Usually, households have similar levels of p_2, but differ to a large extent with respect to the residential moving costs. Note that the sign of $\partial s_1/\partial c_2$ is not determined. In the case that the current commuting time is long, $\partial s_1/\partial c_2$ is positive. In the case that the current commuting time is short, $\partial s_1/\partial c_2$ is negative.

It is however more interesting to examine whether $\partial s_1/\partial z$ increases or decreases if the residential moving costs c_2 increase. A priori, we expect that $\partial s_1/\partial z$ is increasing in c_2. However, it appears that in order to show that Emax is increasing in c_2 one needs the additional assumption that $\partial P_w/\partial c_2 = 0$. Hence, $\partial s_1/\partial z$ may be decreasing in c_2, if $\partial P_w/\partial c_2 < 0$. $\partial P_w/\partial c_2$ is negative if the current commuting time is short, otherwise it will be positive. In conclusion, job search levels of households that face higher residential moving costs will be more responsive to an increase in commuting time given long commuting times. However, given short commuting times, this is not necessarily the case.

Extensions

Mode of transport We have assumed that the instantaneous utility is a function of commuting time that is exogenously given. However, it seems more appropriate to assume that the commuting time is determined by the choice of mode of transport conditional on the given commuting distance. The mode of transport is chosen to maximise instantaneous utility conditional on a budget and time constraint. From a theoretical point of view, search effort and the mode of transport are simultaneously chosen. One may imagine that a worker chooses a faster (but more expensive) mode to spend more time searching for another job. However such an example seems exaggerated in practice. This implies that the worker will determine the optimal search effort, conditional on the chosen mode. Hence, mode of transport and commuting time can be regarded as exogenous determinants of job search behaviour.

Spatial search We have modelled the search process as if jobs and residences arrive randomly from an arbitrary location in space. However, this is not realistic as workers can determine - to a certain extent - where offers will arrive from. This phenomenon is called spatial search (Maier 1995). One expects that workers will search more intensively for jobs near the residential location. We will show that the model can easily be adjusted to accommodate this search behaviour. Let us suppose that worker is able to choose various job search effort levels s_{1d} (and residence search effort levels s_{2d}) to receive job (and residence) offers from region d (d = 1,...,N). Suppose that the distance between the region d and the residential location is increasing in d. Job offers arrive at a rate of $p_{1d}(s_{1d})$, and residence offers arrive at a rate $p_{2d}(s_{2d})$. The expected benefit of an offer, denoted as E_d max, depends on the region from which an offer is generated, since the cumulative distributions F_{wz} and F_{rz} are both decreasing in d. Hence, the lifetime utility given these assumptions can then be written as:

$$\rho V(w,r,z) = v(w,r,z) - \sum_d \{k_{1d}(s_{1d}) - k_{2d}(s_{2d})$$
$$+ p_{1d}(s_{1d})E_d \max[V(w_x,r,z_x) - c_1 - V(w,r,z),0]$$
$$+ p_{2d}(s_{2d})E_d \max[V(w,r_x,z_x) - c_2 - V(w,r,z),0]\}$$

The optimal job search strategy is defined by the choice of s_{1d} (d = 1,...N), characterised by the following first-order equation:

$$\frac{\partial k_1}{\partial s_1} + \frac{\partial p_1}{\partial s_1} E \max[V(w_x,r,z_x) - c_1 - V(w,r,z),0] = 0.$$

The expected benefit of receiving a job offer from a region closer to the residential location is higher than the expected benefit of an offer from a region further away (since F_{wz} is decreasing in d, E_d max is increasing in d). Furthermore, for regions closer to the residential location, it seems plausible that the search costs are less strongly increasing in search effort (for example, international job search is expensive). These considerations imply that the optimal level of job search effort is decreasing in the distance between the region where the worker searches for a job and the residential location.

Finally, it can be shown that workers will increase search effort levels in regions closer to the residential location, and decrease the search effort levels in regions further from the residential location, if residential moving costs increase.

The Data and the Statistical Model

To understand how search effort may depend on the explanatory variables, a logit model is estimated. Thus search effort s^* is defined by $s^* = \beta'x + u$, where x is a vector of explanatory variables and u is logistically distributed. Our data set does not include information about search effort, however it does include information of whether a worker searches or does not search. So s^* is unobservable, but we observe a dummy variable s defined by $s = 1$ if a worker searches for another job, and $s = 0$ otherwise. We suppose that $s^* > c$ if $s = 1$, and $s^* \leq c$ if $s = 0$, where c is a threshold value. The coefficient β can be estimated by Maximum Likelihood. β equals $\partial s^*/\partial x$, so the estimates of β can be interpreted as the effect of a change in x on the amount of search effort s^*.

Our empirical analysis of the probability of being engaged in on-the-job-search is based on a survey called the Interview of the Labour Force ('Enquête Beroepsbevolking'), which was conducted in 1992 (EBB 1992). This survey is representative for the Dutch population. In the current analysis, we use information about the reported search behaviour of 35,450 employed persons who work at least 12 hours per week. Information about search behaviour is included as workers state whether they have been searching for another job during the month preceding the time of questioning. Clearly, the number of observations in the analysis is very large. This has the advantage of measuring the effects of some determinants quite precisely. Another advantage of the data set is that it includes information on commuting behaviour and many other characteristics. Unfortunately, the survey does not include information on the wage level. As a consequence, the effect of all the explanatory variables must be interpreted as the effect on job search, unconditional on the wage. For example, in the case that workers are (partially) compensated for commuting time by receiving a higher wage, the estimated effect of commuting time on job search effort is biased towards zero. Hence, the reported effects of commuting time (and distance) are plausibly stronger than those reported here.

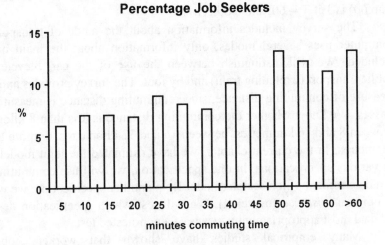

Figure 11.1 Proportion of Job Seekers as a Function of Commuting Time

A large number of variables is available in the EBB (1992) which we use in our empirical analysis to explain variations in search behaviour. We include commuting, job-specific, individual-specific, household-specific, gender-specific and labour-market variables. We also include variables that describe past behaviour. We will focus on a number of variables that determine the commuting costs. The survey includes precise information about the commuting time (measured in minutes). If commuting time exceeds 60 minutes precise information about the commuting time is absent. The aggregate data suggests a strong relationship between the percentage searching and commuting time (see Figure 11.1).

The variables TIME are included which form a spline (see Table 11.1). The coefficient on TIME (0 to 30) is the marginal effect of commuting time on s* when commuting time is less than 30 minutes. The coefficient on TIME (30 to 45) is the marginal effect of commuting time on s* when commuting time is more than 30 and less than 45 minutes. Thus the effect of an increase from 0 to 45 minutes, is 15 times the TIME (30 to 45) coefficient plus 30 times the TIME (0 to 30) coefficient. The TIME (45 to 60) coefficient has an analogous interpretation. The TIME (more than 60) variable is a dummy.

Formally, let T be the commuting time. Then TIME (0 to 30) is min(T,30); TIME (30 to 45) is min(T-30,15) if T = 30, and 0 otherwise;

TIME (45 to 60) is min(T-45,15) if T = 45, and 0 otherwise; TIME (more than 60) is 1 if T = 60, and 0 otherwise.

The survey includes information about the mode of transport. If a commuter uses several modes, only information about the main mode is included. We will distinguish between the use of the car, bicycle, train, public transport (excluding train) and by foot. The survey provides an inexact measure of commuting distance, since commuting distance is measured in 4 classes. We know whether the commuting distance is less than 8 kilometres, between 8 and 16 kilometres, between 16 and 32 kilometres, or more than 32 kilometres. In the current chapter, we have estimated the logit model based on various specifications. In one specification, we will use commuting *time* as a determinant of job search (model I); in another specification, we will use commuting *distance* (model II). We will test which specification describes the data most appropriately by means of a non-nested test.

Many empirical studies have shown that workers' observed commuting times and distances depend on socio-economic variables (Rouwendal and Rietveld 1994, White 1986). One explanation for this phenomenon is that the ability to reduce commuting time (distance) by moving job or residence is varies over different socio-economic groups. An alternative explanation is that the effect of commuting time (distance) on the instantaneous utility varies for socio-economic groups. Hence, one may improve the specification of the empirical model by assuming that a worker reacts to the difference between the worker's commuting time, z, and the average commuting time of the worker's socio-economic group z^*. We will call $z - z^*$ the commuting time gap. In one empirical specification, we allow the workers' search effort levels to vary with the commuting time gap (model IV). Since z^* is unknown, we proxy z^* by the predicted value of z (using a linear regression model and assuming that commuting time is lognormal distributed (Rouwendal and Rietveld 1994). We will compare the results with an empirical specification in which we include commuting time z as a linear explanatory variable (model IV).

In the empirical specifications, we distinguish between four different positions in the household: 1) two-earner households, 2) single person household, 3) wage earner with a partner who is not employed, 4) other members in the household (this group mainly consists of workers who live with their parents). Moreover, we allow for gender-specific households effects. In one specification, we will include interaction effects to test whether gender or household characteristics influence the marginal effect of commuting time on job search (model V).

A large number of individuals-specific job-specific variables is included in the analysis to control for observed heterogeneity of the current job and the commuter. We have included dummies for work at night, work during the evening and work during the weekend, and a dummy for workers who do not have a permanent contract. In addition, the number of hours worked is included and a dummy for those who occupy the job for more than one year. Furthermore, we include measures for the educational level, age, and a dummy for workers who are not born in the Netherlands. We also introduced a number of gender-specific variables: a gender dummy, the number of hours (if female), the number of minor and adult children (if female).

The Empirical Results

In this section, we report and discuss the empirical effects of variables that are directly related to the relationship between job search behaviour and commuting.

We interpret the results as follows (see Table 11.1): The results show that commuting *time* and commuting *distance* both affect job search effort (model I and model II). Hence, although both specifications provide evidence that the journey between the workplace and the residential location affects job search, it is not clear which factor is the main cause. To explore this issue further, we have tested which specification is the most appropriate. Since the two specifications are non-nested, an 'encompassing' test of the two specifications is used. The idea of this test is that a 'full' model is estimated in which both non-nested specifications are nested. Hence, standard Likelihood Ratio tests can be applied. In the case that the 'full' model does not reject one specification and rejects the other specification, the former model encompasses the latter model. It appears that the 'full' model has a loglikelihood of -8102.993; model I has a loglikelihood of -8104.589 and model II has a loglikelihood of -8113.036. Hence, the 'full' model does *not* reject model I at the 5% significance level (LR = 3.192, $\chi^2(3)$= 7.81), where the 'full' model does reject model II at the 5% significance level (LR = 20.086, $\chi^2(4)$= 9.49). Hence, the results indicate that the commuting costs are mainly determined by the implied value of commuting time and less by the monetary costs associated with the commuting distance. For a similar conclusion, Dubin 1991).

We have explained above that according to the search model, it is plausible that the effect of commuting time on search effort is non-linear. In particular, it is expected that the effect is convex, which seems implied by the empirical results (see model I). The marginal effect of commuting time on search effort is constant if the commuting time is less than 45 minutes (about 0.0060). Nevertheless, if the commuting time exceeds 45 minutes, the marginal effect of commuting time on search effort increases sharply (0.0172). To test whether the marginal effect is constant, we have re-estimated the model specifying commuting time as a linear function, see model III (we suppose that commuting time is 60 if commuting time > 60). It appears that the coefficient of commuting time is 0.0090. The latter specification however was rejected at the 5% significance level against model I. As explained above, this result has two explanations. Firstly, the commuting costs (viz. the instantaneous utility function) might be a convex function of commuting time. An alternative explanation is that this result holds because the probability of accepting a job offer is increasing in commuting time *and* the utility of holding the job is decreasing in commuting time.

We are also interested in the elasticities of job search with respect to commuting time. Thus we calculated the expected effect of a highly-educated male who commutes by car and is between 35 and 45 years old. The expected probability of being engaged in job search in a certain month is about 10.0% if his current commuting time is negligible. If the current commuting time of the same worker is about 1 hour, the expected probability of searching would be about 14.8%. Thus the increase in the probability of searching would be about 50%.

The effects of the mode of transport on job search are not very pronounced. However, workers who use public transport (excluding train) search more than other workers. Hence, the costs associated with using public transport seem higher than the costs associated with using other means of transport, even when commuters choose the mode which they prefer (given a budget and time constraint). Moreover, the results point out that workers search the least when they commute by foot (ceteris paribus, commuting time or commuting distance). This makes sense, since the costs of commuting by foot are minimal and many people enjoy walking. Another explanation is that those who commute by foot have very short commuting times (80% of those who walk arrive within 10 minutes) and the specification of commuting time may not be flexible enough. Therefore, we have re-estimated model I by including an additional dummy if the commuting time is less then 10 minutes (the results are not reported in this chapter). Given this more flexible specification of commuting time, the effect of commuting by foot is still statistically significant, whereas the additional dummy is highly insignificant (and even positive). Hence, the latter explanation can be refuted.

Table 11.1 Empirical estimates of coefficients for on-the-job search

standard errors in parentheses; *: significant at 5%.

	model I	model II	model III	model IV	model V
* Travel mode					
Car	-0.07	-0.12	-0.08	-0.08	-0.08
	(0.05)	(0.05)*	(0.05)	(0.05)	(0.05)
Train	-0.20	-0.08	-0.15	-0.14	-0.14
	(0.12)	(0.12)	(0.11)	(0.11)	(0.11)
Foot	-0.31	-0.36	-0.29	-0.28	-0.28
	(0.14)*	(0.14)*	(0.14)*	(0.14)*	(0.14)*
Bicycle	-0.02	-0.02	-0.02	-0.02	-0.02
	(0.10)	(0.10)	(0.10)	(0.10)	(0.10)
Public transport (reference)					
* Commuting time (in minutes)					
TIME (0 to 30)	0.0067				
	(0.0029)*				
TIME (30 to 45)	0.0060				
	(0.0062)				
TIME (45 to 60)	0.0172				
	(0.0084)*				
TIME (more than 60)	0.1684				
	(0.1494)				
Commuting time				0.0090	0.0084
				(0.0015)*	(0.0028)
Commuting time gap				0.0097	
				(0.0016)*	
* Commuting distance					
Commuting distance = 8 (reference)					
8 < commuting distance=16	0.14				
	(0.06)*				
16< commuting distance=32	0.09				
	(0.07)				

Table 11.1 continued

Commuting distance > 32	0.37				
	(0.08)*				

* Interaction effects

Commuting time (if male)				0.0002	
				(0.0028)	
Commuting time (if two-earner household)			0.0007		
			(0.0028)		
Loglikelihood	-8104.589	-8113.036	-8108.976	-8108.258	8106.935

By comparing model III and model IV, it is clear that the effects of commuting time and commuting time gap (the difference between the worker's commuting time and the worker's predicted commuting time) are almost the same. The effect of commuting time gap on job search is only slightly (and insignificantly) larger than the effect of commuting time on job search. This suggests that the marginal effect of commuting time on job search is the same for workers who belong to different socio-economic groups.

We have investigated the latter issue further by incorporating interaction effects. Model V includes commuting time and two interaction effect variables. One variable which is equal to the commuting time if male (and 0 otherwise) and one variable which is equal to the commuting time if the worker belongs to a two-earner household (and 0 otherwise). As can be seen from Table 11.1, the interaction effects do not have any affect. Furthermore, we have estimated many other specifications with other interaction effect variables, and we have specified commuting time in different ways. For all specifications, the interaction effects are statistically negligible. Hence, job search levels of households which face higher residential moving costs do not appear to be more responsive to an increase in commuting time.

Conclusion

In this chapter, we have analysed job search behaviour of employed individuals in the Netherlands. Thus, we have investigated what are the determinants of job search effort. In particular, we are interested in the effect of commuting time - an important component of the commuting costs - on the probability of being engaged in on-the-job search. Rather surprisingly, this topic has received hardly any attention in the economic literature although there is much political concern over the consequences of congestion - and thus commuting time - on the functioning of the labour market. For example, policies which address travel behaviour should preferably take into account that some workers are willing to change job as a result of high commuting time.

We find that commuting time increases the decision to search for another job, whereas commuting distance is of less importance According to the results, the probability of being engaged in on-the-job search increases with about 50% if commuting time increases from zero to one hour. This effect is however not linear. If the workers' commuting time exceeds 45 minutes, the probability of searching for another job increases more sharply. These results, are in line with search theory, which indicates that, plausibly, search effort is convex in commuting time. Rather surprisingly, we do not find any evidence that the relationship between job search behaviour and commuting time differs for various socio-economic groups.

PART V

SUMMARY AND CONCLUSIONS

12. Summary and Implications for Policy

Summary

The main aims of this study have been the following:

(*i*)   to formulate models based on search theory in order to analyse the relationship between job mobility, residential mobility and commuting; and

(*ii*)   to use these models as a basis for empirical research concerning job mobility, residential mobility and commuting.

In light of the aforementioned research aims, the study has been divided into four parts (I - IV):

Part I (chapters 1 - 2)

In part I, we have given a review of state-of-the-art of research about commuting, job and residential moving behaviour. We argued that it may be fruitful to analyse commuting behaviour by focusing on job and residential moving behaviour.

Part II (chapters 3 - 5)

In Part II, we have dealt with the relationship between job and residential mobility and commuting from a theoretical point of view. In chapter 3, an analytical search model has been introduced which aims to highlight the relationship between job mobility, residential mobility and commuting. This model is developed on the basis of recent developments in search theory. An essential element of the model is that it does not rely on any sequential ordering of job or residential moves. This search model is the theoretical foundation of the claim that those with higher commuting costs

167

(measured in terms of distance or time) will move more often job and residence, and will search more for other jobs and residences. One of the basic implications of the model is that workers with relatively high commuting costs tend to expect those costs to only be temporarily borne. It is also argued that the model indicates that in the standard case workers first accept a job and then move residence closer to the new workplace location, although this sequence may be reversed depending on the conditions of the labour and housing market. Finally, according to the search model, job-to-job and residential mobility are independent, conditional on the current commuting costs.

Chapter 4 extends the search model introduced in chapter 3. Here, we focus on the relationship between job mobility, residential mobility and commuting of two-earner households. The case of two-earner households deserves special attention, because the two wage earners share a dwelling but have different working places. For this very common type of household, non-trivial results are obtained. We have clarified that the decision to move (job or residence) is not only influenced by the commuting distance of the other wage earner in the same household, but is also affected by the distance between the workplaces of the two wage earners in the same household. Specifically, both wage earners have higher job mobility rates if the distance between the workplaces is longer. Though it appears to be difficult to compare moving and commuting behaviour for two-earner households and single wage-earners, the search model clearly indicates that generally two-earner households will have lower job mobility rates than single wage-earners.

One of the basic results of the search model introduced in chapter 3 is that workers who may move residence in the future gain more from a simultaneous increase in commuting distance and wages than those who may not move residence. In chapter 5, we have investigated what consequences this may have for the study of commuting behaviour. The major result of this chapter is that it demonstrates that workers voluntarily accept commuting costs which are not compensated for by the current characteristics of jobs and residences. The reason for this is that workers realise that commuting costs are temporary because they may move job or residence in the future. The result that commuters do not demand full compensation for current commuting suggests intuitively that those workers who are more mobile in the housing market demand *less* compensation (in the form of wages) for commuting than others, and are therefore more likely to accept a job offer. We have explained that this intuition is misleading: more mobile workers in the housing market may demand higher wages than those who are not. We also discussed the effect of the geographical structure on commuting behaviour according to the search model. One of the implications of the search model is that if potential employers and dwellings are more homogeneously distributed over space, future job and residence relocations are more important as factors which determine commuting behaviour.[1]

Part III (chapters 6 - 9)

In Part III, we have presented the results of empirical analyses of job and residential mobility in the Netherlands. In chapter 6, we have estimated the effect of commuting distance on job and residential moving using the Telepanel (1992) data set.

In chapter 7, we have laid the foundation of a procedure to estimate the workers① marginal willingness to pay for commuting based on the search model proposed in chapter 3. We have demonstrated that given information on job durations and voluntary job moves, the marginal willingness to pay for commuting can be estimated. Our estimates imply that the marginal willingness to pay to avoid additional commuting time for workers who commute more than half an hour by car or train is about 2/3. However for workers who commute less, the willingness to pay is expected to be lower.

Chapter 8 and 9 draw draws attention to the empirical investigation of the job moving behaviour of two-earner households. The Telepanel (1992) data set provides information on the moving behaviour of two-earner households, which enables us to test the theoretical predictions of the search model that job mobility depends positively on the distance between the working places of the two wage-earners. Although it appears that the number of observations is too limited to draw strong conclusions, we do not find strong reasons to reject the search model. The results imply that two-earner households refuse job offers which would be accepted by single wage-earners because two-earner households are less able than single wage-earners to reduce the commuting distance via a residential move.

Part IV (chapters 10-11)

An attempt to analyse the determinants of commuting distance based on micro data is made in chapter 10. We employ panel data, which may have the advantage that more precise estimates are obtained. Recall that our view is that job mobility, residential mobility and commuting behaviour are simultaneously determined. As a result, we are somewhat more careful to include regressors which are exogenous according to static theories, but endogenous from our point of view. For example, the empirical results support the hypothesis that commuting distance is negatively related to the probability of moving job. Thus workers who are more mobile in the labour market will attain a more favourable situation as time passes. A similar effect of the probability of moving residence on commuting has not been identified. This may support earlier findings that the employment location is more responsive to the residential location than the residential location is to the job location.

One of our policy implications in this chapter is based on the notion that workers search for better jobs and residences. Workers do not choose a residence-job combination which offers a unique optimal commuting distance, but instead accept a wide range of combinations of jobs and residences. Policies which aim to reduce commuting - e.g. policies which reduce the costs of moving residence or moving job - will therefore hardly be effective in the short run. In the long run however, positive effects of these policies are expected because workers may obtain shorter commuting distances at lesser costs.

In chapter 11, we investigate empirically whether employed persons vary job search behaviour with respect to commuting distance, commuting time and mode of transport and a range of other explanatory variables. The empirical analysis is based upon the EBB (1992) data set which provides information about the on-the-job search activities of workers. We find that commuting time strongly increases the decision to search for another job. According to the results, the probability of being engaged in on-the-job search increases by about 50% if commuting time increases from less than ten minutes to one hour. If the worker's commuting time exceeds 50 minutes, the probability of searching for another job increases more steeply. One of the (surprising) outcomes is that search intensity does not depend on the mode of transport.

Implications for Policy

This study provides a theoretical and empirical investigation of job moving, residential moving and commuting behaviour in the Netherlands. This approach has hopefully provided new insights for the reader into the relationship between commuting behaviour and the functioning of the labour and housing market. This kind of research may be of relevance for effective commuting policies, because it provides a theoretical and empirical foundation for the notion that commuting policies aiming to reduce commuting affect the functioning of the labour and housing market. For example, results imply that the effect of commuting time on the search activity is non-linear. If the commuting time exceeds 50 minutes, the probability of searching for another job increases sharply. Those with commuting times more than 60 minutes search about 50% more in the labour market than those who work nearby. Empirical estimates for the marginal willingness to pay for commuting have been provided taking into account that workers may change job and residence.

The demand for commuting is a derived demand in order to spatially connect the labour and housing market. Policies which are formulated in order to reduce the external costs of commuting may thus focus on potential market imperfections in the labour and housing market. In this study it has been explained that those workers who commute more, also move job or residence more often. In the Netherlands, the job moving and residential moving rates are low compared to other developed countries. This suggests that there exist considerable relocation costs and other market imperfections. It may be expected that if some market imperfections in the labour and housing market are removed that commuters will be more inclined to reduce the commuting distance. Thus an obvious policy recommendation is to reduce the costs associated with moving job and residence. For example, in almost all countries which are a member of the European Union, buying a house involves a substantial stamp duty (between 1 and 10% of the value of the house). Pension schemes often imply large costs of changing job.

In the Netherlands, commuting is encouraged by the current tax regime. Given the presumption that it is wise to price external costs however, it is recommended to decrease the moving costs and to increase the current commuting costs per kilometre.[2] These latter costs can be increased by means of a road pricing system, via the worker's income tax or as a tax levied on the employer based upon the commuting distance of the employee. Such a change in the (tax) structure of the economy has the advantage that the external costs of commuting are internalised which gives the right incentives. In addition, the welfare loss due to moving costs is higher than merely the expenses of the moving costs, so a reduction of the moving costs is wise even in the absence of external commuting costs.

This study has also focused on the relationship between residential and job moving decisions and commuting behaviour for two-earner households. Our empirical results suggest that two-earner households move less job than other households and commute more. In addition, the results suggest that two-earner households infrequently move residence. If the results are indeed correct then the anticipated rise in the participation of women in the labour market will reduce the flexibility of the labour and housing market and the commuting distance will increase.

Policies which stimulate workers to search for other jobs in order to reduce the commuting distance may take into account that males and females behave dissimilarly in the labour market. We found that female workers search more for other jobs when they work more hours.[3] This result clearly indicates that females are more responsive than males to the time spent in the labour market - which includes the commuting time. This may imply that females react in different way from men to measures which increase the commuting expenses but decrease the commuting time.

In the current study we have studied the relationship between commuting, job moving and residential moving behaviour. The spatial structure of the economy has received some attention, although maybe not to the extent it deserves. It seems therefore worthwhile to introduce the spatial structure more explicitly in the search model. In the future we will therefore work on an extended urban equilibrium model which explicitly includes search behaviour. Thus far our results suggest that due to suburbanization of firms the average commuting distance will increase, because the increased uncertainty about the (future) workplace will reduce the incentives of workers to reduce the commuting distance by means of a residential move.[4]

Notes

[1] Such a result may be of some importance. Suburbanization of firms is quite common. In particular, the introduction of more new communication technologies in the near future may diminish the benefits for firms to locate near other firms.

[2] We propose the following thought experiment. As a rule of thumb, in the Netherlands, the stamp duty is 6%. The value of the house is about 4 times the yearly net wage and is occupied for about 10 years. So the implied average yearly stamp duty is 2.5% of the annual wage. Given a net wage of 160 guilders a day, this would imply an average daily stamp duty of 4,00 guilders (1 dollar is 20 guilders). The average commuting distance is 20 kilometres (one way), so, on average, a worker commutes daily 40 kilometres. Given these numbers, a government-budget

neutral change in the tax system may involve the abolishment of the stamp duty and the introduction of a commuting tax which would imply a commuting tax per kilometre of about 0.10 guilder. For two-earner households the implied tax would even be the half.

[3] Moreover, females search less if the have minor children and if they have a partner who is employed.

[4] The observation that the average commuting distance in the Netherlands - a country where firms and households are relatively homogeneously distributed over space - is larger than all the neighbouring countries may support this claim (see Jansen, 1992).

Bibliography

Albrecht, J.W., N. Holmlund and H. Lang (1991), Comparative statics in dynamic programming models with an application to job search, *Journal of Economic Dynamics and Control*, 15, 555-769.

Alonso, W. (1964), *Location and land use*, Harvard Univ. Press, Cambridge, USA.

Amemiya, T. (1985), *Advanced Econometrics*, Basil Blackwell, Oxford, UK.

Amemiya, T. (1991), A note on left censoring, Department of Economics, Stanford University.

Amundsen, E.S. (1985), Moving costs and the microeconomics of intra-urban mobility, *Regional Science and Urban Economics*, 573-583.

Anas, A. (1982), *Residential location markets and urban transportation: economic theory, econometrics and policy analysis with discrete choice models*, Academic Press, New York.

Arnott, R. A. de Palma and R. Lindsey (1990), Departure time and route choice for the morning commute, *Transportation Research B*, 24, 209-28.

Arnott, R. A. de Palma and R. Lindsey (1994) The welfare effects of the congestion tolls with heterogeneous commuters, *Journal of Transport Economics and Policy*, 28, 139, 61.

Ashenfelter, O. and J. J. Heckman (1973), The estimation of income and substitution effects in a model of family labor supply, *Econometrica*, 42, 73-85.

Banister, D. (1993) Policy responses in the UK, in *Transport, the Environment and Sustainable Development*, eds D. Bannister and K. Button, London: E and FN Spon.

Bartel, A.P. (1979), The migration decision: what role does job mobility play?, *American Economic Review*, 69, 775-786.

Bartels, C.P.A. and K.L. Liaw (1983), The dynamics of spatial labor mobility in the Netherlands, *Environment and Planning A*, 15, 329-342.

Bartik, T.J., J.S. Butler and J.T. Liu (1992), Maximum score estimates of the determinants of residential mobility: Implications for the value of residential attachment and neighborhood amenities, *Journal of Urban Economics*, 32, 233-256.

Beesley, M.E. and M.Q. Dalvi (1974), Spatial equilibrium and the journey to work, *The Journal of Transport Economics and Policy*, 8, 197-222.

Black, M. (1981), An empirical test of the theory of on-the-job search, *Journal of Human Resources*, 16, 129-140.

Boehm, T.P. (1981), Tenure choice and expected mobility: a synthesis, *Journal of Urban Economics*, 10, 375-389.

Brown, L.A. and J. Holmes (1971), Search behavior in an intraurban migration context: a spatial perspective, *Environment and Planning*, 3, 307-326.

Burdett, K. (1978), Employee search and quits, *American Economic Review*, 68, 212-220.

Burdett, K. (1981), A useful restriction on the offer distribution in job search models, in G. Eliasson, B. Holmlund and F.P. Stafford (eds.), *Studies in labor market behavior: Sweden and the United States*, Stockholm, Sweden: I.U.I Conference Report.

Burdett, K., and R. Wright (1994), Two-sided search, paper presented at the summer school Microeconomics of the labour market, Paris, La Sorbonne.

Burdett, K. and D. T. Mortensen (1978), Labor supply under uncertainty, Ronald G. Ehrenberg, ea., *Research in labor economics*, vol. 2, 109-158, Greenwich, Conn., JAI Press.

Burgess, S.M. (1992), A search model with job changing costs: 'euroslerosis' and unemployment, *Oxford Economic Papers*, 44, 75-88.

Butler, J.S. and R. Moffit (1982), A computationally efficient quadrature procedure for the one-factor multinomial probit model, *Econometrica*, 50, 761-764.

Camstra, R. (1994), Household relocation and commuting distance in a gender perspective, PDOD-paper No. 26, University of Amsterdam.

Chamberlain, G. (1984), Panel data, in *Handbook of Econometrics*, vol II, Z. Griliches and M. Intriligator (eds.), 1247-1318, Amsterdam, North-Holland.

Chesher, A.D. and T. Lancaster (1983), The estimation of models of labour market behaviour, *The Review of Economic Studies*, 50, 609-624.

Clark, W.A.V. and M. Kuijpers-Linde (1994), Commuting in restructuring urban regions, *Urban Studies*, 31, 465-483.

Clark, W.A.V. and R. Flowerdew (1982), A review of search models and their application to search in the housing market, in W.A.V. Clark (ed), *Modelling housing market search*, Croom Helm, London.

Clark, W.A.V. and T.R. Smith (1982), Housing market search behavior and expected mobility, theory 2: the process of search, *Environment and Planning A*, 14, 717-733.

Clark, W.A.V. and W.F.J Van Lierop (1986), Residential mobility and household location modelling, in *Handbook of Regional and Urban Economics, vol. I*, P. Nijkamp (ed.), 97-132, Amsterdam, North-Holland.

Clark, W.A.V., J.O. Huff and J.E. Burt (1979), Calibrating a model of the decision to move, *Environment and Planning A*, 11, 689-704.

Clayton, D. (1978), A model for association in bivariate life tables and its application in epidemiological studies in familial tendency in chronic disease incidence, *Biometrika*, 65, 141-151.

Clayton, D. and J. Cuzick (1985), Multivariate generalizations of the proportional hazards model, *Journal of Royal Statistical Society Series A*, 148, 82-117.

Cogan, J.F. (1981), Fixed costs and labor supply, *Econometrica*, 49, 945-963.

Cox, D.R. and D. Oakes (1984), *Analysis of survival data*, Chapman Hall, London.

Crane, R. (1996), The influence of uncertain job location on urban form and the journey to work, *Journal of Urban Economics*, 37, 342-56.

Curran, C., L.A. Carlson and D.A. Ford (1982), A theory of residential location decisions of two-worker households, *Journal of Urban Economics*, 12, 102-114.

De Jong, G.F. and R.W Gardner (eds.), *Migration decision making: multidisciplinary approaches to microlevel studies in developed and developing countries*, Pergamon Press, New York.

Devine, T.J. and N.M. Kiefer (1993), The empirical status of job search theory, *Labour Economics*, 1, 3-24.

Doeringer, P.B. and M.J. Piore (1971), *Internal labor markets and manpower analysis*, Heath Lexington Books, Massachusetts.

Dubin, R. (1991), Commuting patterns and firm decentralization, *Land Economics*, 67, 15-29.

EBB (1992), Enquête Beroepsbevolking, Centraal Bureau voor de Statistiek, Heerlen.

Eckstein, Z. and K.I. Wolpin (1989), The specification and estimation of dynamic discrete choice model, *Journal of Human Resources*, 562-598.

Elbers, C. and G. Ridder (1982), True and spurious duration dependence: The identifiability of the proportional hazard model, *Review of Economic Studies*, 49, 403-410.

Emmerink, R.H.M., P. Nijkamp, P. Rietveld and J.N. van Ommeren (1996), Variable message signs and radio traffic information: an integrated empirical analysis of drivers' route choice behaviour, *Transportation Research A*, 30, 135-153.

Engelsdorp Gastelaars, van R. and J.C. Maas-Drooglever Fortuijn (1985), Personeel op drift: hoe reageren personeelsleden op een verplaatsing van hun bedrijf?, *Geografisch tijdschrift*, 19, 181-191.

European Conference of Ministers of Transport (1990), *Transport policy and the environment*, Paris: ECMT/OECD.

Evers, G. and Veen, A. van der (1986), *Pendel, migratie en deelname aan het beroepsleven, macro- en micro- economische benaderingen*, PhD thesis, Febo, Enschede.

Evers, G.H.M. (1990), The residential location and workplace choice: a nested multinomial logit model in: Fischer, M.M., Nijkamp, P. and Y.Y. Papageorgiou (eds.), *Spatial choices and processes*, North-Holland, Amsterdam.

Flinn, C.J. and J.J. Heckman (1982), Models for the analysis of labor force dynamics, in R.L. Basmann and G.F. Rhodes (eds.), *Advances in econometrics, Vol. 1*, JAI Press, Greenwich, CT.

Ginsberg, R.H. (1979a + b), Timing and duration effects in residence histories and other longitudinal data I +II, *Regional Science and Urban Economics*, 9, 311-331 and 369-392.

Gleave, D. and M. Cordey-Hayes (1977), Migration dynamics and labour market turnover, *Progress in Planning*, 8, 1-95.

178 *Commuting and Relocation of Jobs and Residences*

Gordon, P., Kumar A., and H.W. Richardson (1989), The influence of metropolitan structure on commuting time, *Journal of Urban Economics*, 26, 138-151.

Graves, P.E. and P.D. Linneman (1979), Household migration: theoretical and empirical results, *Journal of Urban Economics*, 6, 383-404.

Greenwood, M.J. (1980), Metropolitan growth and the intrametropolitan location of employment, housing, and labor force, *The Review of Economics and Statistics*, 62, 4, 491-501.

Greenwood, M.J., P.R. Mueser, D.A. Plane and A.M. Schlottmann (1991), New directions in migration research, *The Annals of Regional Science*, 25, 237-270.

Gritz, R.M. (1993), The impact of training on the frequency and duration of employment, *Journal of Econometrics*, 57, 21-52.

Gronberg, T.J. and W.R. Reed (1994), Estimating workers' marginal willingness to pay for job attributes using duration data, *The Journal of Human Resources*, 24, 911-931.

Hall, R.E. (1982), The importance of life time jobs in the U.S. economy, *American Economic Review*, 72, 716-724.

Hamilton, B.W. (1982), Wasteful commuting, *Journal of Political Economy*, 90, 1035-1053.

Hamilton, B.W. (1989), Wasteful commuting again, *Journal of Political Economy*, 97, 1497-1504.

Hardman, A.M. and Y.M. Ioannides (1995), Moving behavior and the housing market, *Regional Science and Urban Economics*, 25, 21-39.

Hartog, J. and H. van Ophem (1994), On-the-job search and the cyclical sensitivity of job mobility, *European Economic Review*, 38, 802-808.

Hartog, J., E. Mekkelholt and H. van Ophem (1987), Een empirische studie naar de arbeidsmobiliteit in Nederland, OSA werkdocument nr. W 32.

Hartog, J., E. Mekkelholt and H. van Ophem (1988), Testing the relevance of job search for job mobility, *Economics Letters*, 27, 299-303.

Hey, J.D. and C.J. McKenna (1979), To move or not to move, *Economica*, 46, 175-185.

Holmlund, N. and H. Lang (1985), Quit behavior under imperfect information: searching, moving, learning, *Economic Inquiry*, 23, 383-393.

Holzer, H. J. (1991), The spatial mismatch hypothesis: what has the evidence shown?, *Urban Studies*, 28, 105-122.

Holzer, H. J. (1994), Work, search and travel among white and black youth, *Journal of Urban Economics*, 35, 320-345.

Honoré, B.E. (1993), Identification results for duration models with multiple spells, *The Review of Economic Studies*, 60, 241-246.

Hougaard, P. (1986), Survival models for heterogeneous populations derived from stable distributions, *Biometrika*, 73, 387-396.

Hougaard, P. (1987), Modelling multivariate survival, *Scandinavian Journal of Statistics*, 14, 291-304.

Hsiao, C. (1986), *Analysis of panel data*, Econometric society monographs no. 11, Cambridge University Press.

Huff, J.O. (1984), Distance-decay models of residential search, in G.L. Gaille and C.J. Willmott (eds.), *Spatial statistics and models*, D. Ridels Publishing Company, 345-366.

Hughes, G.A. and B. McCormick (1985), An empirical analysis of on-the-job search and job mobility, *Manchester School*, 53, 76-95.

Hwang, H. D., W.R. Reed and C. Hubbard (1993), Compensating wage differentials and unobserved productivity, *Journal of Political Economy*, 100. 4, 835-858.

Imbens, G.W. (1994), Transition models in a non-stationary environment, *The Review of Economics and Statistics*, 4, 703-720.

Ioannides, Y.M. (1987), Residential mobility and housing tenure choice, *Regional Science and Urban Economics*, 17, 265-287.

Jansen, G.R.M. (1992), Commuting in Europe: homes sprawl, jobs sprawl, traffic problems grow, Delft, INRO-TNO INRO-VVG, 1992-13.

Kahn L. and S. Low (1982), The relative effects of employed and unemployed search, *Review of Economics and Statistics*, 64, 234-241.

Kahn L. and S. Low (1984), An empirical model of employed search, unemployment search and nonsearch, *Journal of Human Resources*, 19, 104-117.

Kalbfleisch, J.D. and R.L. Prentice (1980), *The statistical analysis of failure time data*, Wiley, New York.

Kasper, H. (1983), Toward estimating the incidence of journey-to-work costs, *Urban Studies*, 20, 197-208.

Kiefer N.M. (1988), Economic duration data and hazard functions, *Journal of Economic Literature*, 646-679.

Killingsworth, Mark R. (1993), *Labor supply*, Cambridge University Press.

Kim, S. (1992), Search, hedonic prices and housing demand, *The Review of Economics and Statistics*, 74, 503-508.

Kooreman, P. and J. Rouwendal (1992), Search behaviour and the Dutch housing market: a structural model, Wageningen.

Lancaster, T. (1979), Econometric methods for the duration of unemployment, *Econometrica*, 47, 936-956.

Lancaster, T. (1990), *The econometric analysis of transition data*, Cambridge University Press.

Lindeboom, M. (1992), *Empirical duration models for the labour market*, thesis publishers, Amsterdam.

Lindeboom, M. and G.J. van den Berg (1994), Heterogeneity in models for bivariate survival, the importance of the mixing function, *Journal of Royal Statistical Society Series B*, 56, 1, 49-60.

Lindeboom, M. and J.J.M. Theeuwes (1991), Job duration in The Netherlands: The co-existence of high-turnover and permanent job attachment, *Oxford Bulletin of Economics and Statistics*, 53, 243-264.

Linneman, P. and P.E. Graves (1983), Migration and job change: a multinomial logit approach, *Journal of Urban Economics*, 14, 263-279.

Maddala, G.S. (1985), Limited-dependent variable models using panel data, *Journal of Human Resources*, 22, 3, 307-338.

Madden, J.F (1981), Why women work closer to home, *Urban Studies*, 18, 181-194.

Maier, G. (1995), *Spatial search, structure, complexity, and implications*, Studies in contemporary economics, Physica-Verlag Heidelberg.

Mallar, C.D. (1977), The estimation of simultaneous probability models, *Econometrica*, 45, 1977-1988.

Marshall, A.W. and Olkin, I. (1967), A multivariate exponential distribution, *Journal of American Statistical Association*, 62, 30-44.

McCall, J.J. (1970), Economics of information and job search, *Quarterly Journal of Economics*, 84, 133-146.

McGinnis, R. (1969), A stochastic model of social mobility, *American Sociological Review*, 33, 712-722.

McKenna (1985), *Uncertainty and the labour market; recent developments in job-search theory*, Harvester Press.

Mekkelholt, E.W. (1993), *Een sequentiele analyse van de baanmobiliteit in Nederland*, PhD thesis, Amsterdam.

Meurs, H (1991), *A Panel data analysis of travel demand*, PhD thesis, Groningen.

Meurs, H, Kockelkoren, M and J. Jager (1991), Paneldata analysis van vervoerwijzekeuze; theorie, in: P.T. Tanja (ed.) Colloquium Vervoersplanalogisch Speurwerk -1991-De prijs van mobiliteit en van mobiliteitsbeperking, Delft.

Meurs, H. and P. Bovy (1992), Nieuwe baan of ander huis: verandering van vervoerwijze?, paper presented at Colloquium Vervoersplanalogisch Speurwerk 1992, Rotterdam, 26-27 November.

Mortensen, D.T. (1986), Job search and labor market analysis, in O.C. Ashenfelter and R. Layard (eds.), *Handbook of Labor Economics*, Amsterdam, North-Holland

Muth, R.F. (1969), *Cities and housing*, Chicago, The University of Chicago Press.

Nickel, S.J. (1979), Estimating the probability of leaving unemployment, *Econometrica*, 47, 1249-1266.

Nijkamp, P. and P. Rietveld (1982), Soft econometrics as a tool for regional discrepancy analysis, *Papers of the Regional Science Association*, 49, 3-21.

Nijkamp, P., Pepping, G and D. Banister (1996), *Telematics and transport Behaviour*, Springer-Verlag, Berlin.

Oakes, D. (1982), A model for association in bivariate survival data, *Journal of Royal Statistical Society Series B*, 44, 414-422.

Ophem, van H. (1991), Wages, nonwage job characteristics and the search behavior of employees, *The Review of Economics and Statistics*, 145-151.

ORIN (1984), Relatievormen in Nederland 1984, Klijzing, F.K.H., D.J. v.d. Kaa and N.W. Keilman et al., Amsterdam, Steinmetzarchief.

Pickles, A.R. and R.B. Davies (1991), The empirical analysis of housing careers: a review and a general statistical modelling framework, *Environment and Planning A*, 23, 465-484.

Pickles, A.R. Davies, R.B. and Crouchley, R. (1982), Heterogeneity, non-stationarity and duration of-stay effects in migration, *Environment and Planning A*, 14, 615-622.

Pissarides, C.A. (1994), Search unemployment with on-the job search, *Review of Economic Studies*, 61, 457-475.

Pissarides, C.A. and J. Wadsworth (1994), On-the-job search: some empirical evidence from Britain, *European Economic Review*, 38, 385-401.

Pivvs (1992), Nieuwe baan of ander huis: verandering van vervoerwijze?, Pivvs, Ministerie van Verkeer en Waterstaat.

Ravenstein, E.G. (1885), The laws of migration, part I, *The Journal of the Royal Statistical Society*, 48, 167-227.

Ridder, G. (1984), The distribution of single spell duration data, in Neumann, G. and Westergard-Nielsen, N. (eds.), *Studies in Labor Market Dynamics*, Springer Verlag, Berlin, 45-73.

Ridder, G. (1990), The non-parametric identification of generalized accelerated failure-time models, *Review of Economic Studies*, 57, 167-182.

Rietveld, P. (1993), Policy responses in the Netherlands, in *Transport, the Environment and Sustainable Development*, eds. D. Banister and K. Button. London: E and FN Spon.

Rima, A. and L.J.G. van Wissen (1987), *A Dynamic model of household relocation: A case study for the Amsterdam Region*, Free University Press, Amsterdam.

Roseman, C.C. (1971), Migration as a spatial and temporal Process, *Annals of the Association of American Geographers*, 61, 589-598.

Rosen, S. (1974), Hedonic prices and implicit markets: product differentiation in pure competition, *Journal of Political Economy*, 82, 34-55.

Rossi, P. (1955), *Why families move*, The Free Press, Glencoe, IL.

Rouwendal, J. (1991), Housing Choice and Search Behaviour in a Disequilibrated Market: An exploratory Analysis, *Kwantitatieve Methoden*, 12.

Rouwendal, J. (1992), Ruimtelijke interactiemodellen en zoektheorie, Wageningen.

Rouwendal, J. (1994), Spatial labor markets and commuting, 34th Congress of the Regional Science Association, Groningen, August, 1994.

Rouwendal, J. (1995), Spatial Job search and commuting distances of female workers, Wageningen.

Rouwendal, J. and Rietveld P. (1988), Search and mobility in a housing market with limited supply, *Annals of Regional Science*, 22, 3, 80-98.

Rouwendal, J. and Rietveld P. (1994), Changes in commuting distances of Dutch households, *Urban Studies*, 31, 09, 1545-1557.

Seater, J. (1979), Job search and vacancy contracts, *American Economic Review*, 69, 411-419.

Shaw, R.P. (1975), *Migration, theory and fact: A review and bibliography of current literature*, Regional Science Research Institute, Philadelphia.

Sickles, R.C. and P. Taubman (1986), An analysis of the health and retirement status of the elderly, *Econometrica*, 54, 1339-1356.

Siegel, J. (1975), Intrametropolitan migration: a simultaneous model of employment and residential location of white and black households, *Journal of Urban Economics*, 2, 29-47.

Simon, H. (1957), *Models of man*, New York, Wiley.

Simpson, W. (1980), A simultaneous model of workplace and residential location incorporating job search, *Journal of Urban Economics*, 8, 330-349.

Singell, L.D. and J.H. Lillydahl (1986), An empirical analysis of the commute to work patterns of males and females in two-earner households, *Urban Studies*, 23, 119-129.

Sjaastad, L.A. (1962), The costs and returns of human migration, *Journal of Political Economy*, 70, 80-93.

Small, K.A. (1992), *Urban Transportation Economics*, Fundamentals of Pure and Applied Economics, Harwood, Chur.

Smith, T.R. and F. Mertz (1980), An analysis of the effects of information revision on the outcome of housing market search, with special reference to the influence of realty agents, *Environment and Planning A*, 14, 681-698.

Smith, T.R. and W.A.V. Clark (1982), Housing market search behavior and expected mobility, theory 1: measuring preferences for housing, *Environment and Planning A*, 14, 681-698.

Smith, T.R., Clark, W.A.V., Huff J. and P. Shapiro (1979), A decision-making and search model of intra-urban migration, *Geographical Analysis*, 11, 1-22.

Speare, A., S. Goldstein and W.H. Frey (1975), *Residential mobility, migration and metropolitan change*, Cambridge, Mass, Ballinger.

Steinnes, D.N. (1977), Causality and intraurban location, *Journal of Urban Economics*, 4, 69-79.

Stigler, G. (1961), The economics of information, *Journal of Political Economy*, 69, 213-225.

Stigler, G. (1962), Information in the labor market, *Journal of Political Economy*, 70, 94-105.

Sugden, R. (1980), An application of search theory to the analysis of regional labour markets, *Regional Science and Urban economics*, 10, 43-51.

Theeuwes, J., M. Kerkhofs and M. Lindeboom (1990), Transition intensities in the Dutch labour market 1980-1985, *Applied Economics*, 22 1043-1061.

Van den Berg, G.J. (1992), A structural dynamic analysis of job turnover and the costs associated with moving to another job, *The Economic Journal*, 102, 1116-1133.

Van den Berg, G.J. (1994), The effects of changes of the job offer arrival rate on the duration of unemployment, *Journal of Labor Economics*, 12, 3, 478-498.

Van den Berg, G.J. (1995), Wage dispersion and mobility, *Economic Modelling*, 12, 1, 15-27.

Van den Berg, G.J. and C. Gorter (1997), Job search and commuting time, *Journal of Business and Economic Statistics*, 15, 269-281.

Van den Berg, G.J. and M. Lindeboom (1994), Attrition in panel data and the estimation of dynamic labor market models, working paper, CREST, no 9436.

Van den Berg, G.J., J.N. van Ommeren and Cees Gorter (1996), Search theory and the relation between job durations and willingness to pay for job attributes, Free University, mimeo.

Van den Berg, G.J., M. Lindeboom and G. Ridder (1994), Attrition in longitudinal panel data and the empirical analysis of dynamic labour market behaviour, *Journal of Applied Econometrics*, 9, 421-435.

Van der Schaar, J. (1991), *Volkshuisvesting: een zaak van beleid*, Spectrum, Utrecht.

Van Dijk, J. (1986), *Migratie en arbeidsmarkt*, PHD thesis, van Gorcum.

Van Dijk, J., H. A.M., Folmer, Herzog H.W. Jr., and A.M. Schlottman (1989), *Migration and labor market adjustment*, Kluwer Academic Publishers, The Netherlands.

Van Ommeren, J.N. and G. Russo (1995), Are vacancies difficult to fill?, *Applied Economics*, 29, 349-357.

Van Ommeren, J.N., Rietveld, P. and P. Nijkamp (1994), Job mobility, residential mobility and commuting: a theoretical and empirical analysis using search theory, TI Discussion Paper, Vrije Universiteit, Amsterdam, 94-145.

Van Ommeren, J.N., Rietveld. P. and P. Nijkamp (1995), Are job-to-job and residential mobility related?, TI Discussion Paper, Vrije Universiteit, Amsterdam, 95-10.

Van Ommeren, J.N., Rietveld, P. and P. Nijkamp (1996), Residence and workplace relocation; a bivariate duration model approach, *Geographical Analysis*, 28, 4, 315-329.

Van Ommeren, J.N., Rietveld. P. and P. Nijkamp (1998), Spatial moving behaviour of two-earner households, *Journal of Regional Science*, 38, 1, 23-46.

Van Ommeren, J.N., (1996), *Commuting and relocation of jobs and residences; a search perspective*, Thesis Publishers, NR 130, Amsterdam.

Van Ophem, H. (1991), Wages, nonwage job characteristics and the search behavior of employees, *The Review of Economics and Statistics*, 71, 145-151.

Van Ours, J. (1990), An international comparative study on job mobility, *Labour*, 4, 3, 33-55.

Van Wee, G.P. (1996), Ruimtelijke en mobiliteitsreacties van werkenden op bedrijfsverplaatsingen;resultaten van empirisch onderzoek, RIVM.

Vanderkamp, J. (1971), Migration flows, their determinants and the effects of return migration, *Journal of Political Economy*, 79, 1012-1032.

Verhoef, E.T. (1994), External effects and social costs of road transport, *Transportation Research A*, 28, 273-84.